CONCILIUM

Religion in the Eighties

CONCILIUM

Concilium 146 (6/1981): Project 'X'

WHERE DOES THE CHURCH STAND?

Edited by

Giuseppe Alberigo

and

Gustavo Gutiérrez

English Language Editor
Marcus Lefébure

T. & T. CLARK LTD.
Edinburgh

THE SEABURY PRESS
New York

June 1981
T. & T. Clark Ltd., 36 George Street, Edinburgh EH2 2LQ
ISBN: 0 567 30026 9

The Seabury Press, 815 Second Avenue, New York, N.Y. 10017
ISBN: 0 8164 2313 X

Library of Congress Catalog Card No.: 80 54388

Printed in Scotland by William Blackwood & Sons Ltd., Edinburgh

Concilium: Monthly except July and August.
Subscriptions 1981: All countries (except U.S.A. and Canada) £27·00 postage and handling included; U.S.A. and Canada $64.00 postage and handling included. (Second class postage licence 541-530 at New York, N.Y.) Subscription distribution in U.S. by Expediters of the Printed Word Ltd., 527 Madison Avenue, Suite 1217, New York, N.Y. 10022.

CONTENTS

v

Part III
The Reception of Vatican II in a Changed Historical Context

Bulletins

Erratum

Concilium 145, page 49:
Translator's name should have read Ruth Murphy.

Editorial

ON THE threshold of the Eighties we thought it worth while reflecting on the present state of the Church. We wanted to make an appreciation of the Christian churches, above all of the Catholic Church, as they are today.

Although we had made no attempt to furnish an exhaustive description, either phenomenologically or with an eye to the lines of development, preparing this issue led us to recognise even more clearly the complex state of present Church life.

In some instances it is a matter of confused or even contradictory situations, but in other and more frequent instances we are presented with a richness of life, authentic gospel manifestations and ferments that bear witness to a generous availability to the impulses of history, by means of which men and churches are called to conversion.

To many it will seem easier to emphasise the gaps in the panorama sketched by the various articles than to make use of the contribution they make. Nonetheless we think such an attempt is to be made and that it succeeds in the measure that, beyond providing important data for our knowledge and evaluation, it affirms the need for a 'critical' analysis (that is, a rigorous analysis rationally deployed) of the Churches as they are today.

In recent decades more than one synthetic interpretation of the Church's condition has been suggested. J. Maritain has dreamt of a new Christianity, Cardinal Suhard has professed the Church's youthfulness, John XXIII has proclaimed a new season for the cultivation of the Church understood as 'garden', I. Illich foresaw the crisis of the Seventies, warning against a levelling out on the model of the multinationals. Lastly, J. Delumeau raised a cry of alarm that is at the same time an act of hope: Is Christianity dying?

This collection of material does not aim at offering a new 'diagnosis', to stand side by side with those just mentioned. Instead it hopes to contribute to gaining acceptance for the need to have an adequate reading of the Church's life. This life is an indispensable setting for theological reflection, absolutely necessary for the very understanding of history in the light of faith. All too often the study of ecclesial life is smothered in narrow boundaries, is subjected to a disturbingly empirical account, reducing itself to 'ecclesiastical' matters, losing sight of the far more complex depth of ecclesial reality.

In selecting this requirement of an adequate reading there is no intention of ignoring that a 'critical' reading of the life of the Church has limits as well as positive aspects. The most glaring limit is the rational level adopted by such a reading, since we thereby opt out of attaining a level of faith. As Christians we realise that this is the most decisive level for discovering where the Church of the Lord Jesus *really* is when considered in the economy of salvation, but as men engaged in study we accept the duty of recognising with humility the limits of the means of knowledge at our disposal.

In the last decade intolerance for reflection on the Church has grown more intense so that theology has busied itself with other matters—Christology, above all—and the attention of Christian public opinion has turned towards issues more directly bearing on faith and its meaning in a secularised world. Very often it has been a question of salutary reactions to the ecclesiocentrism that had prevailed in the preceding decades. In some cases, however, such a reaction has led to a disinterest in theory and a withdrawal from action on the part of many of those involved. We feel we must distance ourselves from this position, not only on general grounds but also and above all because of a precise reason related to the Church as it is today.

In fact looking at the increasingly more detailed picture of Churches in different areas, cultures and socio-economic conditions, interest in a full ecclesiological account varies in intensity and degree. That is, it seems to us that there are areas where Christianity has been established for many centuries (the 'Atlantic' belt), secularisation is very advanced, and the socio-political conditions (neo-capitalism and representative democracy) guarantee even to those less well-off acceptable standards of living. Here attention to the problems of the Church's conception and organisation diminishes because of the small historical impact of the Church, integrated in the total ordering of society. The Church occupies an increasingly marginal position, and finds it hard to be a place of prophetic announcement and thus of hope and expectation.

The biggest difference, however, between the Church as it was at the end of the nineteenth century and as it is at the end of this century is precisely its dissemination outside this area, in increasingly diversified historical conditions. In the countries of eastern Europe as in the Soviet Union, in Latin America as in Asia, Christians undergo experiences far different from those to be had in the Atlantic belt. and it is in those very Churches—from Poland to Brazil—that Christians cannot and do not want to give up a creative reflection in the Church and on the Church. A theological reflection, this, that unites the essential biblical givenness with the signs of the times emerging from the depths of history through the painful struggles of the poor.

We think that in all these places—amounting to at least half of the present geographical map of Christianity—Christian reflection as a re-understanding of the gospel message solicited by what has to be done in history has—and can have to an even greater extent—a living context in the Church, involved in the history of men that seek liberation in the truth. Here not only can neither the Church nor the close theological examination that concerns it be eclipsed or made marginal, but there is a need which cannot be postponed to serve the active faith of millions of men and women with an ecclesiology that helps the churches to be always more faithful to the vocation which the Spirit expresses through historical events.

For these Christians to be able to live their faith joyfully in the Church is a vital necessity, and from this the entire universal Church can gain a priceless measure of youthfulness.

We know that 'ecclesiology' is an ambiguous term to the extent that in the development of 'Latin' theology it has often stood as an equivalent to ecclesiocentrism, expressing feelings of power and self-affirmation by the Church in and over society. In terms of this perspective Vatican I has said all that could be said, and more. With Vatican II a radical change got underway, something to be developed with patience and in freedom; but such a change cannot simplistically resolve itself into a refusal to reflect on the Church. More fruitful, if more demanding, is to search for new ways of bringing this about in a manner matching the gospel awareness of the Christian communities as they are today.

GIUSEPPE ALBERIGO
GUSTAVO GUTIÉRREZ

Translated by Robert Ombres

PART I

Long-term Factors

Henri-Marie Féret

The Word of God and its Sovereignty in Today's Church[1]

FOR THE believer, the sovereignty of the Word of God is first and foremost a datum that depends on the absolute nature of the mystery of God. In this instance, we have to go back to the clear statements in the Bible about the sovereign word or *dabhar* of the creator, used eight times in Gen. 1:1-2:3, the oracle of the later Isaian prophet in Isa. 55:10-11, the Word that is not fettered, even if the prophet who proclaims it is (2 Tim. 2:9), the prologue to Heb. 1:1-3 and above all the inexhaustible prologue to the gospel of John and the inclusio between 1:1, which speaks of the Word that is in God and relative to God (*pros ton theon*) and is God, and 1:18, the Word made flesh among men and revealing the mystery of God whom no one has ever seen. Speaking of the sovereignty of the Word is therefore to speak of the sovereignty of God who always has, in Jesus Christ, the Word made flesh in our history, not only the last word, but also the first and the last letter (Alpha and Omega, Rev. 1:8; 21:6; 22:13).

If God addresses his Word to men, it is clearly necessary for them to receive it with the greatest lucidity possible, to say nothing of the joyful freedom that the truth brings for action. At the end of revelation, the gospel of John teaches that freedom and truth are Jesus himself (8:32, 36; 14:6), precisely because he is the Word of God. Speaking of the sovereignty of the Scriptures is first and foremost to say how one sees them in relation to Jesus—they all speak of him (John 5:39-40). Secondarily, it is to say what place they have in the economy of revelation and what part they must therefore play in the life of faith.

Revelation is not given to us as a theodicy, a moral theology, or an ecclesiology, but as a history. It has developed as a single unit and it continues to be handed on in a network of concrete realities in a situation of constant becoming, the relativity of which, in other words, the relationship between different aspects of man's history, must be respected in any interpretation that bears the sovereignty of the Word of God in mind. I would like to go a little more deeply into this question here.

As the Second Vatican Council reminded us (*Lumen Gentium*, § 7), the life of the Church in the time in which man's history is unfolded is eschatological. This is of great importance in biblical revelation and I shall return to it later. The Word of God which illuminates the Church in its march through history with its divine light and the Spirit which animates the Church by placing it in communion with the eternal presence of God himself are both eternal values which ensure and can ensure the unity of the living

3

tradition of the people of God only through the continuous presence of man's history. It is in that constantly changing history that the Church must always discern the eternal presence of God for the recapitulation of all things in Christ and the Spirit (Eph. 1:10). This is essential to the Church's eschatological nature. It is what the eternal Word does through the Church 'always, to the close of the age' (Matt. 28:20). It is the redeeming incarnation of that Word in the new and eternal covenant, an understanding of which the Spirit of Pentecost gives the Church day after day (John 16:7-15), on condition that it listens to that Word that is given to it in the Scriptures that are entirely concentrated on Jesus, the Messiah and the Son of the living God. It is therefore in those Scriptures that the Church must first and foremost look for an answer to the questions that the continuous presence of history asks of faith, if it wants those answers to be the leaven in human history of its own progress, that is, the true leaven of the kingdom of God (Matt. 13:33) and not the ephemeral leaven of the Pharisees or of Herod (Mark 8:15). What, then, is there in the present life of the Church of this sovereignty of the Scriptures?

That sovereignty should obviously be recognised and proclaimed. Following Leo XIII (*Providentissimus*, 1893), Benedict XV (*Spiritus Paraclitus*, 1920), John XIII (in his homily when he took over Saint John Lateran as his cathedral on 23 November 1958) and the Second Vatican Council (*Dei Verbum*, 1965, § 24), John-Paul II reminded us of this sovereignty in his Apostolic Letter written on the centenary of Saint Basil (*Doc. Cath.*, No. 1780, 17 February 1980). Such statements of principle are, however, not enough. What is there in the teaching of faith by the Church's ministers and therefore in that teaching as experienced by all Christians? Is there respect in the life of the Church for the sovereignty of the Scriptures and the Word of God (leaving fundamental hermeneutics aside for the moment), both in ordinary religious instruction and in the Church's response to the questions raised by faith? In all honesty, we are bound to give a negative answer to this question and indeed it seems to be less and less respected in discussions about the life of the Church and the Churches (with the result that ecumenism is at present making very slow progress). There were two dogmatic constitutions promulgated by the Second Vatican Council and one of them, *Dei Verbum* on Divine Revelation, is almost a dead letter in all these discussions.

There is, however, one exception and I shall point later on to its importance and to its weakness. This was the great step forward made liturgically in that Catholics were able to hear the Bible read—four centuries after the Reformers had called for it—in their own languages. (However controversial the translations may be.) This partly accounts for the increasing interest even among the most ordinary Christians in Scripture and their disappointment when members of the clergy, who are often hardly better prepared to hear it as the Word of God than they are, discourage them by referring back to them questions which are in any case for the most part oversimplified and which are asked by specialists in the literary and historical criticisms of the Bible who fail to appreciate the demands made by integral hermeneutics.

Apart from this increase in interest in the Bible in the basic communities of the people of God, however, there is less and less emphasis on biblical theology and on revelation itself in the ordinary teaching of faith. The categories which increasingly form the basis for this teaching are the earlier scholastic theology and, even more often, the human sciences that are dominant in society today. These include sociology, psychology and other modern sciences that are often controversial in the light of reason. A vague claim is often made that the authority of the Bible can be used to justify many of the affirmations made by this modern form of catechesis, whereas in fact no support can be found in the gospel. Frequently, for example, a text is quoted and its meaning is radically changed as in the case of the beatitude: 'Blessed are those who are persecuted for righteousness' sake' (Matt. 5:10). Here 'righteousness' or 'justice' (*dikaiosune*) points to the perfection of the 'righteous', in the strictly biblical sense of the word, but in modern catechesis, this is applied to the political and social struggle against injustice of various kinds in modern society and used as an invitation to the Church and its members to take part in that struggle. There is a certain ambiguity in the vocabulary of 'Justice and Peace'.

The answers given to the fundamental questions that confront the Christian in his faith today hardly ever come from a firm return to revelation contained in the biblical tradition understood in the light of appropriate hermeneutics. All the churches agreed to accept these hermeneutics based on concrete and historical theology on 17 October 1973 in a meeting with Paul VI and Professor Skydsgaard. To take only one example, none of the documents published by the Roman Curia is based on teachings of biblical revelation as distinct from a few texts taken out of context, and that in order to explain the problems that urgently confront Christian faith in the first place in hermeneutics and then in Christology, ecclesiology, anthropology and Christian ethics. They also try to respond to the demands made by the new relationship between the Church and the world, the pastoral urgency of which was clearly stressed by *Gaudium et Spes*. Several theologians are at present at the centre of serious controversy and the mass media have naturally enough given prominence to this situation to the great delight of the public. It is, however, remarkable that hardly any part at all is played in this controversy by the Word of God in biblical revelation, which is in this case not questioned at all rigorously. The theologians who are concerned with these problems are not looking for an answer to their questions in the revelation of the Word, but in the human sciences that are so dominant in society today. Existentialism and structuralism play a leading rôle in hermeneutics. Sociology and especially the Marxist analysis of society are used to interpret man's collective existence even in the churches. Psychology and above all Freudian psychology is applied to the study of ethics.

The theologians who are opposed to this kind of interpretation—and these are above all those scholars whose texts are published by the Roman congregations and are therefore invested with all the authority of Peter's successor—base their opposition on theologies that are no more dependent on the revelation of the Bible than those theologies that they themselves are criticising. In fact, their own theologies are an extension of earlier teachings which can hardly be reconciled with the teachings of Vatican II. To take only one example, there is the problem of eschatology (see *Lumen Gentium*, § 7), which the editors of a recent publication (1979) on the 'last things' would find very difficult to justify by appealing to biblical revelation, especially if they wanted to do full justice to the literary genres of Scripture.

In questions such as these, it is most important to go back to the clear traditional distinction that should always be made between three levels of Christian thought:

the level of biblical revelation, which is, in the last resort, the only divine norm for faith, provided that questions are asked with the help of hermeneutics that are as homogeneous as possible with the economy of biblical revelation. That economy is both concrete and historical and has nothing to do with a rational dialectical analysis; the level of dogmatic definitions and especially those of the Church's ecumenical councils, which set up the landmarks of the living Christian tradition in human history and asks us simply to bear in mind the relative nature of their formulations, which are conditioned by the culture of the period; the level of theologies, which are human studies of faith and are valuable to believers (and to the witness that those believers bear in the world) only in so far as they continue to be dependent on the levels of biblical revelation and dogmatic pronouncements. In their attempts to elucidate the new problems that confront believers in their understanding of faith and their bearing witness to faith, the Church's theologies are above all dependent on biblical revelation.

The present crisis of faith is so serious that, for the first time in the history of the Church, all emphasis is placed firmly on this third level. This is true even if we take account of the nominalism of the fourteenth and fifteenth centuries, which was the first stimulus leading Christians back to the Scriptures and eventually to the breakaway of the Protestant Reformers. This division is still important, because it has lasted so long, to anyone who reflects about history in the light of biblical revelation.

In these theological discussions, it is most important not to lose sight of one fact which ought to be seen as more significant than all others, in view of the loss of faith among the people of God, who ought to form the Church. More and more members of that people of God, in all cultures and at all levels, are unsure of what is revealed by God and of what claims their faith. They no longer know what is God's word and what is only man's word, a word which may be theological and which may point to the past or suggest new ways in the future.

The Church is first and foremost a community of faith. It is only secondarily a community of charity and a community of liturgical cult centred on the Eucharist (see Acts 2:42). Its numbers are decreasing from day to day (see, for example, the statistics of the Institute of Statistics set up by Paul VI in the Secretariat of State—Catholics apparently comprised fewer than 18 per cent of the world's population in 1978). This decline in numbers can be explained in the first place as the result of a crisis of faith caused by the reasons that I have just given. Luther correctly said that the Church was born of the Word of God and for this reason he also believed that *bonum esset Ecclesiae si Porphyrius natus non fuisset cum suis universalibus*. The 'universals' of today are not those of nominalism, but those of the human sciences. These all have the effect of alienating the Church from the Word of God, with the result that the crisis of faith continues to become worse, because faith is not nourished by the Word that cannot be replaced by any human words, even theological ones. 'You search the Scriptures, because you think that in them you have eternal life, and it is they that bear witness to me; yet you refuse to come to me that you may have eternal life' (John 5:39-40). By way of antithesis, Jesus also cursed the scribes who rejected the Word of God and replaced it with their human traditions (see Mark 7:6-13 par; going back to Isa. 29:13 LXX). The gospels of Luke and John both insist on the need to know Scriptures in order to believe in the resurrection of Christ (see, for example, Luke 24:13-32; 24:44-47; John 20:9). That resurrection is, of course, at the heart of Christian faith.

The mystery of the evil opposition to Christ that characterised not only the scribes, but also the leading priests and elders is a phenomenon that is found at all times. In history, however, it was concentrated in the Sanhedrin consisting of the Jewish scribes, elders and priests who decided to have Jesus put to death and who obtained that death from Pilate, without realising the universal foundations for that decision in the sin of the world (see Matt. 23:36; Luke 3:17; 1 Cor. 2:8, etc.). It would not be wrong to think that there are very many such scribes today among the Church's theologians and exegetes. The hermeneutics of the best of these exegetes are limited to literary and historical criticism. They make use of these two essential kinds of criticism and go beyond them, but they do not go so far as to discern the intentions of Christian teaching and the pastoral inspirations in which the charisma of the divine inspiration of the scriptural authors plays a part. These intentions and inspirations have enabled these texts to be the permanent bearers of God's revelation to his people.

There are also at the moment very many different forms of hermeneutics, resulting in a heterogeneous interpretation of the different literary genres of the Bible, replacing literary and historical criticism by analyses based on the human systems developed by Marxist, Freudian, existentialist and structuralist thinkers. The historian would regard the anachronisms involved in this method amusing if there were no serious consequences for the faith of the people of God. The most obvious of these consequences is that those who follow these systems look for and find in Scripture everything that they want to find except the Word of God, which should, by the very nature of Scripture itself, be given to the Church. It is fortunate that they have not yet gone so far as to question the traditional canon of Scripture, since this can only be justified by integral hermeneutics.

It is inevitable that theologians who work in this way should move further and further away from the primary sources of their science—sources to which theology should remain very close if it is really seeking to understand faith. These theologians look for guidance in the human sciences of the new culture that is at present trying to discover itself in the world and is therefore confronting the Church's faith with many new problems. It is consequently inevitable that their theologies will suggest answers to these problems which are more dependent on the human sciences that have presented them than on the faith that they challenge. Most of the time too, the historian will recognise that these answers lag well behind a fashion or a generation in comparison with the rapid growth of these human cultures within our rapidly changing modern society.

The launching of an international review of theology—*Concilium*—was proposed during the last session of the Second Vatican Council and I welcomed this idea wholeheartedly. I believed then that the line followed by the Council should be continued and that the historical ecumenical encounter that took place on 17 October 1963 would first of all imply a return to the study of Scripture and the Fathers of the Church. I should like now to suggest that the editors of *Concilium* should devote at least one issue of the journal to drawing up a systematic account of all of the issues that have appeared so far. This balance sheet should show two sides. On the one hand, it should provide a list of the contributions devoted to the human sciences and to the critical questions—in both senses of the term—that are presented by those sciences to faith. On the other hand, it should also contain a list of contributions devoted to an examination of the Scriptures and not to those theologies that are only remotely related, if related at all, to Scripture.

This balance sheet would undoubtedly reveal the minimal contribution made in the journal to an attempt to discover what divine revelation really is and what it is not in the Church's teaching and to penetrate the thick historical and cultural layers that have formed around that revelation and have therefore made it almost inaccessible to believers. In the course of history, the churches and their theologies have become an increasingly impenetrable screen between the Word of God and believers, although, if they are correctly understood, the Scriptures are always quite contemporary and able to bear witness in each generation to Jesus the Messiah and Son of the living God.

Many readers will think that this diagnosis is too severe, but there is already a great deal of evidence in the churches that points to its correctness. If it is accepted, it is clear that all the efforts to renew religious teaching both among adults and among children and young people—attempts which are of necessity dependent for their success on the degree of theological training and skill that prevails among the clergy at all levels—can only deepen the crisis of faith that exists among the people of God and weaken the witness that they bear in the world.

Can the situation be put right and in the first place the situation in the all-important sphere of hermeneutics? In the present predicament, which problems in the life of the Church should be approached first?

The evolution of ecclesiology, which began with *Lumen Gentium* and which is the most vital contribution that the Council made to the living fabric of the Church, must continue. The Church does not consist primarily of those who minister to the people of God, but of those who are baptised and who are on the way towards baptism. The

Church's ministers are dedicated, by 'ordination' as deacons, priests or bishops, to the service of the people of God, who are not there simply to obey their ministers. This was one of the points on which Jesus, the founder of the apostolic institution, insisted most of all in the case of the Twelve. He even stressed its importance within the framework of the Last Supper (Luke 22:24-27). *Lumen Gentium* marked a big step forward in the direction of a return to this fundamental ecclesiological datum of the New Testament. It would only have been better if the order of Chapters 3 ('The Hierarchical Structure of the Church') and 4 ('The Laity') had been reversed and if Chapter 3 had been entitled 'Ministries in the Church'. We have, then, to continue the development that began with the document and speak in the first place of the lay people and then of the ministers who are 'ordained' to the apostolic service that Jesus specified and wanted them and all those who were to bear witness to the New Testament after him to perform.

It is therefore most important that we should begin by shifting the centre of gravity in the Church from the institutional level of a Church of clergy—this is borne out by the word 'Church' itself in the way in which it is still commonly used: 'The Church teaches . . .', 'The Church commands . . .', 'The Church forbids . . .', etc.—to the level of concrete, evangelical and brotherly communities. The teaching contained in Chapter 3 of *Lumen Gentium*, which is to some extent based on the earlier ecclesiology of the Church (as outlined in the Code of Canon Law of 1917), has readjusted the balance between the successor of Peter (and the centralisation of Rome which has continued to grow since the time of Gregory VII) and the episcopate. Despite this, however, the priority of the clergy of all ranks has still been preserved. It is therefore very significant for the institution that the idea of 'collegiality' has been singled out in this chapter to the exclusion of almost everything else and that there has been a proliferation in the Church of synods, commissions, conferences, sessions and so on, all vying with each other for the title of collegiality. At the same time, practically nothing remains now of the sacramental aspect of the episcopate, which, while making the individual bishop personally responsible for that part of the Christian community that had been entrusted to his care, also often made it necessary for him to keep at a distance from what was decided by those commissions that claimed to be 'collegial' and of which he was a member. It was precisely this kind of thing that emphasised the administrative centralisation of the Church that the Council aimed to reduce so that evangelisation should be closer to the basic communities. This closeness was not regarded as dangerous in itself. On the contrary, it was seen as necessary for the unity of the Catholic community.

If this fact is contrasted with the decreasing membership of the people of God, it becomes more and more obvious that the centre of gravity in the Church must, as I have already said, be shifted without delay from the social and institutional level at which it is at present to the communal level at which the Church will inevitably be forced to live if the present imbalance between the demographic growth of the world and the demographic decline of the Church continues. Because of this development, it will have to consist of concrete evangelical and brotherly communities on a human scale and it will also have to be less of a hierarchically structured world-wide institution. It will consist of modest but authentic living cells acting as leaven in the many different collective groupings in the modern world 'till it is all leavened' (Matt. 13:33). This marks the end of one period of Christianity and the beginning of a new phase in the history of the Church 'until he comes again'.

It is at this level that the whole people of God should without delay be taught about 'the eschatological nature of the pilgrim Church and its union with the Church that has already entered the eternity of the living God' (*Lumen Gentium*, § 7: the real title is 'the heavenly Church'). The present time, dating from Jesus' paschal sacrifice and Pentecost, is the eschatological time in the sense in which it is described in Enoch 1:2 and the whole Christian community, both laity and clergy, should therefore be experiencing the present in the history of the world as the eternal present of the living God. It should also experience that present of the living God as a living in the resurrected Jesus who sends the Spirit and who is at the centre of the revelation of Scripture. The more completely the Christian community lives in this eternal present, the more capable it will be of throwing its light and the strength on each of the successive present times in the history of the end of time and on all the perpetually new questions raised by these present times. This is why the risen Christ (and not the Christ before his Easter experience) gave the Eleven an 'understanding of the Scriptures' by inviting them not to begin their ministry in the period inaugurated by his resurrection until the Spirit of Pentecost had given them 'from above' the power to carry out this eschatological mission (Luke 24:45-49). This could only be done on the basis of concrete communities on a human scale, in which those who have in fact been baptised or who are approaching it perhaps with hesitation or are being prepared for it and those whose task is to minister to the community as ministers of the Word of God are in much closer communion with each other than the members of a Church in the sense of an institution could ever be. In the Church as an institution, institutional values are inevitably accompanied by religious individualism on the part of its members and an isolation of its ministers, who become no more than officials with a function who can be transferred from one unit of the people of God to another at the end of a short term of office.

It should be noted that it is not simply a question here of being more faithful to the New Testament teaching about the Church (although this is quite important in itself). It is that the future of the Church has never before appeared 'at the base' in so many and in such vigorous nuclear communities as it is appearing today. One of the most impressive signs of the presence of the Holy Spirit in the Church today is the apparently spontaneous multiplication of very varied 'communities', some of them unfortunately threatened with anti-clericalism. This sign is also one that points to the Church's future and the Church's ministers should give particular attention to it. There is otherwise a danger that serious changes will be introduced into these communities by the 'enemy' of the parable (Matt. 13:24-30 and 36-43).

It is hardly necessary to add that this shifting of the centre of gravity in the Church from the institutional level to the level of interpersonal Christian communities will strengthen rather than minimise man's consciousness of the universal unity of the Church. These basic communities are already experiencing a need for closer mutual links with each other and, as a whole, with the Roman community, especially since the latter has begun to assume an aspect that is different from the one that it had in the past, that of a centralised administration that it was not always easy to love.

Let us now consider another problem that is closely connected with this one. Those who are responsible for 'vocations' in the Church are very unhappy because, as they say, there are none. No one is coming forward to serve in the Church as a minister. Every aspect of the Church's ministries that can be entrusted to lay people is consequently entrusted to them and their responsibilities are taken very seriously. Yet these lay people are not given any training for the work, nor are they given the necessary graces of 'ordination' for the ministries with which they are entrusted. The people of God are asked to storm heaven with prayers for vocations and those that are given are received with gratitude, even though there may be doubt as to whether the Church will obtain in this way the ministers that it needs. In the meanwhile, the crisis continues to become worse. The statistics prove this—both those relating to the intake into seminaries and those of ministers' requests to be reduced to the lay state. These ministers do not want to find themselves in an abnormal situation with regard to canon law, but they are still anxious to belong to the Christian community and still claim to believe in Christ. The Lord established the apostolic institution in and for the sake of his Church and he

B

promised to be with it in all its needs—and its need of ministers is of primary importance—'to the close of the age'. Would he, then, forget his Church or at least its apostolic institution?

More than twenty years ago, the results of an inquiry into this crisis of vocations caused great consternation in the Church. The seminaries were emptying and fewer and fewer students were entering the Church's orders. In response to this publication, I wrote a note for *La Vie Spirituelle* (No. 446, January 1959) drawing attention to the theological distinction between vocations to practise the evangelical counsels, which go back to the supernatural prudence given to all believers in accordance with the demands made by their state in life, and vocations to the presbyterate (or, as I wrote at the time, the priesthood), which were concerned with the needs of the Church's communities and therefore the responsibility of the pastors of those communities who called—or did not call—suitable subjects to help them in their ministry. As soon as this note appeared in print, the highest authorities of the Assembly of the Cardinals and Archbishops of France (there was no General Assembly of the French Episcopate at that time) intervened and told my superiors that nothing should follow this note. The only effect of an article or articles would be to empty the seminaries still further.

I therefore did not publish the article that I had already begun to write. In it, I had tried to show in greater detail that this distinction between the two types of vocation was both completely traditional and based on the ecclesiology of the New Testament. The seminaries continued to empty with an even greater speed, despite the fact that my article did not appear in print. I still have the file containing the correspondence about this question. It throws an interesting light on the theological opinions of those in authority at the time in the French Church in the matter of vocations.

Charles Péguy maintained that there were two kinds of authority: the authority of commandment and the authority of competence. The first called for obedience and condemned man to silence. At that time, I obeyed and was silent. I do not believe that this was of help to the seminaries in their search for candidates for the ministries that were required by the Christian communities. The authority of competence calls and gives preference to all men in a communal search for the truth that will set men free because it has the name of Jesus Christ (see John 8:32 and 36).

The crisis of vocations has continued to become worse. I may therefore be permitted, after more than twenty years of silence, to say once again that the Church will be able to find its way out of this dead-end only by recognising the truth of that distinction between two types of vocation. In addition, it is clear now that we must also go back, in this question as in so many others, to the Word of God as contained in Scripture. We must not persist in handing on those entirely human words that Jesus condemned as the lasting evil brought about by those scribes who rejected the Word of God and replaced it with their human traditions.

There is first and foremost a need to examine critically and to reform the whole of our Church vocabulary on the basis of the language of the New Testament. 'Hierarchy'—does this mean a hierarchy of commandment or of service (see Luke 22:24-27)? 'Magisterium'—is this an 'infallible magisterium' gratuitously determining the truth on the basis of a 'tradition' that is divorced from Scripture? The Second Vatican Council rejected this dualism when it rejected the theory of the two sources and insisted that Scripture had come about and had been preserved in and for tradition. Scripture is the source and the criterion of that tradition and the only means by which it can continue to be renewed in explicit statements which have the primary task of showing clearly that they are directly dependent on biblical revelation. Jesus asked his disciples not to let themselves be called master, father or teacher, since he, as the Christ and as such inseparable from the Father and the Holy Spirit, was the master and teacher of his disciples (Matt. 23:8-10). Besides which, the text of Luke 10:16, which is often cited in support of blind obedience (I call it this because of its refusal to see in the biblical revelation the basis of what is said), should be understood in the whole of Lucan catechesis to refer to the apostolic teaching interpreting Scripture (see Luke 24:27, 32, 44-47; John 5:39; 20:9, etc.). The unquestionable infallibility of the Church and of Peter and his successors at the centre of the Church means that the whole Church is infallible in so far as its faith is based on the solid rock that was promised to the apostle at such time as he might be converted (Luke 22:32), and in regard to everything that he said, by reference to his profession of faith in the only rock on which the Church could be built—Jesus himself, the Messiah and the Son of the living God (Matt. 16:16-19; 1 Cor. 3:11), at the centre of Scripture.

It is essential to go beyond the current way of speaking about vocations to the apostolic ministries and reconsider the deep and special nature of these ministries on the basis of the ecclesiology that is divinely guaranteed by the New Testament. In the present situation, in which the Christian communities are becoming an increasing minority in the world, what I said in 1959 about the nature of these vocations to the ministries (the diaconal, presbyteral and episcopal ministries) has an even greater urgency today both with regard to the ecclesiology of the New Testament and with regard to the pressing needs of the Christian communities, if the latter are to remain faithful to the Church of Christ.

This whole question is closely related to the criteria used for the selection of ministers, the part played on the one hand by the communities and on the other by their pastors in this choice of ministers, the theological, pastoral and liturgical training of those who are called, the way of life that they should follow in a world that is no longer predominantly Christian and many other factors. Because of these factors, their vocation to the various ministries should not be confused with the call that all Jesus' disciples receive to be perfect in freely following the evangelical counsels. This practice of the evangelical counsels must, I stress, be free, since it would be contradictory to speak of a counsel that is obligatory. No person or institution has the right to make what the Lord left to the free decision of the individual an obligation. The pastors responsible for making the decision may, of course, have to choose between a subject who has freely chosen, without any pressure exerted by the institution or any other form of pressure, to live according to the counsel of voluntary continence and has therefore decided to renounce his right to found a family and another subject who has already undertaken the obligations of the holy state of marriage. In that case, provided that each subject is otherwise equal with regard to his qualities as a minister, the first will probably be preferred because he has greater freedom of action.

What are these ministerial qualities? A minister who is to serve a Christian community should have a clear and solid faith and sound pastoral judgment. He should also be generous in his devotion to that community and have a good reputation among non-believers. If he is married, his life should bear witness to his faithfulness to his wife and his good upbringing of his family. A married subject with these qualities would certainly be preferable to a celibate who is lacking in judgment and who has remained unmarried because he is unconsciously self-centred or for some other reason. The pastoral epistles of Saint Paul—this is not the place to discuss the directly or indirectly Pauline origin of these documents—are full of highly contemporary comments on this question of the criteria that should be used by communities and their pastors in assessing vocations to the ministries.

Following Acts 2:42, the Church that is required not only by the modern world, but also by the world, at every period of human history will be built up on basic communities existing on a human scale and with close interpersonal relationships. In this way, it will become, as I have already said, a number of living cells forming a Church acting as leaven and not simply a 'Church of Christendom'. The more completely this pattern is realised, the more fully those who are baptised and the 'catechumens' on their way towards baptism will be able to participate in liturgical assemblies centred on the Eucharist in a non-individualistic way. The same also applies to all the sacraments. In the light of the Word of the apostles, in the *koinonia* of charity over which the pastors preside (Saint Ignatius) and in the fervour of celebrating liturgies which are not only beautiful in themselves, but which also deepen the inner life, these sacramental assemblies are bound to become once again the Church acting out the new and eternal covenant.

The whole of the liturgical renewal initiated by the Second Vatican Council must find at this centre of community life the source of all useful and necessary adaptations of the sacramental disciplines ranging from baptism to the Eucharist. Let us briefly review those aspects that seem to be the most important in restoring the sovereignty of the Word of God to a position of respect.

The *Ordo poenitentiae*, published on 2 December 1973, marks a timid opening of doors in its reintegration of the sacrament of penance into the life of the community by encouraging public services of penance. Since then, however, the doors thus opened have closed again and there has been a noticeable return to preconciliar attitude and theologies in many different spheres. This return is very disconcerting for any theologian who is conscious of the depth of Christ's teaching about salvation. This teaching forms an essential part of the New Testament and Paul fought and suffered for it. I would like to confine myself here to my own evidence, which is certainly not improvised, and say simply this. First, there is no real sign at present of an energetic return to the divine revelation made in the New Testament of man's complete redemption brought about by the Saviour Jesus Christ, the Messiah and the Son of the living God, and communicated in baptism to all who receive that sacrament and renewed again and again in each Eucharist. Secondly, there is as yet no widespread recognition of the distinction that was made until the twelfth century and was solidly based on biblical revelation. This is the distinction between private sins committed from day to day and the multiform personal penance done by the sinner in the presence of his God on the one hand and, on the other, public sins which are the business, within the Christian community, of those who are responsible for discipline within that community and for ensuring the visible and public authenticity of that community in the unbelieving world. Thirdly, there is no evidence of a return to an institutionalised penitential discipline which changes according to the time and place and which includes public excommunication that would vary in severity according to the seriousness of the public fault, public punishment, again of varying severity, to be undergone by the penitent and finally public sacramental reconciliation.

The present tendency is therefore to return to the individual practice of the sacrament. This is spiritually more tyrannical than the commandments of the Mosaic law (unless it becomes as routine a matter as it was in the quite recent past). It is also anachronistic in that it goes back to the Fourth Lateran Council of 1215 (Chapter 21). It can in fact be no more than an unsatisfactory compromise to give temporary life to a sacrament that is clearly, according to most observers, almost entirely without a future. Neither the community nor its members are likely to benefit from it.

I have only mentioned here what seem to me to be the most important aspects. I would like to conclude by stressing once again that only an energetic return to biblical revelation, in other words, to the sovereignty of God's Word as contained in Scripture, will ensure the authenticity of the Church's life. Without an authentic inner life, the Church will not be able to bear effective witness in a world in which it is and will continue for some time to be a minority.

There are many patristic texts which indicate the constant concern of the Church

Fathers to make no statement to their fellow-Christians in their pastoral ministry that could not find support in the sovereignty of Scripture, which was for them not only unique, but also beyond dispute. I will, however, confine myself to one case, in which Saint Augustine displayed scrupulous concern. Before commenting on the second half of verse 13 in Ps. 85 (Vulgate translation): 'Thou hast delivered my soul from the depths of Sheol', the Bishop of Hippo warns his listeners about the way in which they will receive his hesitations: 'Do not become excited, brothers, if what I am going to tell you is not presented as something of which I am certain, since I am a man and, in so far as I am able to do so, I can only dare to say what comes from the Scriptures and nothing from me (*nihil a me*)'.

These final words may be an affirmation of a fact or they may express a desire to make a firm decision, but the essential meaning is the same in both cases: Because he is only a man, Augustine is not bold enough to say anything that does not, in his opinion, express with certainty the Word of God as contained in Scripture. In this particular case of Ps. 85:13b, he does not know whether *nephesh* ('soul') points in the language of the Bible to the living being and not to the soul as distinct from the body and whether Sheol denotes the subterranean extension of the grave and death and not hell in the sense in which he understood it (and in which we are still sometimes expected to understand it). For this reason, he is hesitant about the meaning of this phrase 'lower hell' or 'depths of Sheol'. He therefore suggests two different interpretations, which cannot be considered here, and then returns to his point of departure: 'I would like to conclude by saying, brothers, that, whether (the meaning of this text) is this or that, you should regard me only as someone who searches (*scrutatorem*) the Word of God, not someone who (is not sure of the meaning of some of his texts and) is bold enough to make an affirmation' (*Enarr.* in Ps. LXXXV, 13, § 17; CCL, XXXIX, 1966, pp. 1189-1191).

Both for believers whose faith has ultimately only one object and content—the Word of God—and even more for those members of the apostolic institution who are responsible for the ministry of that Word, respect for its sovereignty has a positive and a negative content. In the positive sense, it is asking Scripture to 'set them on the path of the truth' (Hippolytus *Daniel* (Sources chrétiennes 14, 1943) I, XXXI, 4, p. 125). This includes the replies to the questions that each new generation and each new culture can and must ask them. In the negative sense, it is not being bold enough (as Augustine said) to give replies that will only be human and therefore disappointing and even harmful in their contradictory claims which, perhaps unconsciously do violence to the liberating sovereignty of the Word of God.

Translated by David Smith

Note

1. The editors of this issue of *Concilium* thought that it would be of interest to publish, under this heading, part of the text that the author submitted in response to the first draft outline of this issue.

Marie-Dominique Chenu

The New Awareness of the Trinitarian Basis of the Church

'THE NEW thing is what the resurrection of Christ brings; it is the paschal mystery, which is to be explained in terms not of the past but of the future.

'God comes into the world, as though to meet it. He is out ahead, and he calls. He disturbs. He sends. He creates growth. He liberates. Every other god is a false god, an idol, a dead god; and it is high time our modern consciousness buried him. This multiform god, who inhabits the "old" consciousness of mankind, is in effect behind man, like a cause; he commands, organises, brings man back, and finally alienates him. There is nothing prophetic about him; on the contrary, he is always following behind, as the ultimate reason for the inexplicable, or the last refuge of the irresponsible. This false transcendent being is as old as death. . . .

'By contrast, the new creative force comes into the world along with the world. It does not have to discover itself or prove itself. It reveals itself. It may be accepted or rejected, but it comes as a happening. . . .

'It is the action of the Holy Spirit which brings this new thing into the world. Without him, God is far away, Christ is in the past, the gospel is a dead letter, the Church is a mere organisation, authority is domination, mission is propaganda, worship is a magical evocation, and Christian action is a slave morality.'

This is what Mgr I. Hazim, at that time Metropolitan of Latakia (Syria) and today Patriarch of the East, had to say at the General Assembly of the World Council of Churches at Uppsala in 1968, on the subject of the permanent renewal of Christianity.

We cannot fail to notice, behind this provocative condemnation of the deism of present-day spirituality, the expression of the Trinitarian theology of the eastern Church, according to which the circumincession of the Father, Son and Holy Spirit takes place in the Unity of the Mystery, and thus establishes the Church in history.

1. EASTERN THEOLOGY AT THE COUNCIL

Although it was perhaps less obvious than some others, an important strand in the long reflection which took place at Vatican II was the growing influence of eastern theology at those points at which it offers a different understanding of the faith from

14

Latin theology. This has nothing to do with the often bitter controversies which, in the course of history, have set the two theologies and the two Churches in opposition. There was no hint of such controversies at the Council, and the dialogue with Orthodoxy has wiped out the memory of them. It was by their original presentation of the mystery of God and its manifestations that the eastern prelates exercised a growing influence. In the field with which we are concerned in this article, Trinitarian personalism subtly and effectively reduced the deism to which western thought (including even the concepts used in Vatican I) had more or less succumbed. Some traces of it remained in the texts produced by the preparatory Commission for Vatican II, where the Trinitarian revelation had not succeeded in imparting its characteristic sense and tone to the various statements which had been prepared. The doctrine itself was fully affirmed, it is true, but it was not worked out in the forms in which spiritual truth was conceived and expressed.

The first break-through occurred in the discussion on revelation, when the text of the project entitled *De deposito fidei pure custodiando* met with opposition. This text, though very careful in its dogmatic formulations on the Word of God, failed to establish the Word as in itself the locus of communion with God and the object of personal faith. Mgr Guano, who reported on the schema, declared: 'In this schema concerning the Word of God, it must be a question not only of expressing truth and nurturing the understanding, but also of representing the living and loving God who wants, by way of the human spirit, to reach, touch and penetrate the whole man in his capacity for creation and life.'

Starting from the first sessions in November 1962, many criticisms were raised, and it became apparent that, despite the confidence with which it had been put forward, the project would be rejected. One of the most forceful of the criticisms was that of Mgr Hakim, Greek-Malchite Bishop of Akka. 'It is true', he said, 'that the schema contains riches and values of Latin theology, and we are glad to pay warm tribute to the magnificent *intellectus fidei* which this theology has won for the Church. But we are sorry that the writers of the documents have completely ignored eastern catechetical teaching and theology—those of Cyril of Jerusalem, Gregory of Nazianzus and Gregory of Nyssa, Maximus and John of Damascus—thus steering the universal faith in the direction of their own particular theology, and presenting as conciliar truth what, though it may be a valid expression of the revelation of God, is nevertheless a local and partial one. In eastern theology, where the liturgy is the effective locus of the transmission of the faith, where initiation takes place within the sacramental mystery and not in abstract instruction, devoid of symbol, the mystery of Christ is set forth directly as an *economy*, which is unfolded in history, prepared in the Old Covenant, effected in Christ, realised in the era of the Church. Theoretical explanations, however legitimate and necessary they may be, are never separated from the fabric of Scripture and the testimony of the Fathers. This concrete character of the Word of God reveals its presence in the world. The Church, the Body of Christ, is precisely the authentic place and the living guardian of its transmission.' In an additional note, not read during the sessions, Mgr Hakim continues: 'Western theologians have always a tendency to modalism (and today, alas, to "deism", see catechisms and manuals): an *abstract* God, subjected to analysis by reason; not the living God, in whom the inaccessible mystery of the Father (*theologia*) is revealed by and in the Son, and communicated to men in history (*oikonomia*) through the presence of the Spirit. The Latins neglect, in fact, the reality of this concrete presence in time, and hold to an abstract doctrine. So it is with the schema which has been presented.' The schema was rejected, as everyone knows.

When in 1964 the text of the constitution *De Revelatione* underwent a final revision, several eastern fathers again intervened. We may quote the remarkable contribution of Mgr Edelby on the interpretation of Scripture, all the more notable in that it expresses the spiritual and theological communion existing between members of the Orthodox and Catholic Churches, since it had been prepared and proposed by Mgr Scrima, personal representative of Patriarch Athenagoras. 'The aim of Christian exegesis', he said, 'is to interpret Scripture in the light of the risen Christ, as the Lord himself encouraged the apostles to do (Luke 24). Scripture is a liturgical and prophetic reality, a proclamation before it became a book, the testimony of the Holy Spirit to the event of Christ, which finds its fullest expression in the Eucharistic liturgy. It is by this testimony of the Spirit that the whole Economy of the Word reveals the Father. Post-Tridentine controversy has seen Scripture as primarily a written norm; the eastern Churches see it as the consecration of the history of salvation under the form of human words, inseparable from the Eucharistic consecration, in which the whole of history is summed up in the Body of Christ. . . . For this consecration an epiclesis is necessary, and that is the sacred Tradition. Tradition is the epiclesis of salvation history, the theophany of the Holy Spirit, without which history remains incomprehensible and Scripture a dead letter.'[1]

In the course of these same sessions, from the western side Cardinal Meyer had declared: We are glad that at last we have a living, dynamic, global conception of Tradition, that it is no longer restricted to doctrinal formulations, and that it extends to the liturgy and *praxis* of the Church. We agree that it should be said that it is developed not only through definitions by the *magisterium* but also through the contemplation of the faithful and through inner experience of spiritual things. In short we approve of the declaration which affirms that Tradition grows and develops, while the Church, following the example of the Virgin Mary, keeps in her heart what she has received.'

2. THE RE-AWAKENING OF THE SPIRIT

It would certainly be profitable to follow, in contemporary theology, the application of this high doctrine, particularly with reference to the dogmatic constitution *De divina Revelatione* ('Dei Verbum'). But in line with the purpose of this issue, we shall apply ourselves rather to showing how the concrete life, the experience, the *praxis* of the Church have been nourished by this Trinitarian insight, too long neglected by the Latins.

Let us say at once that this analysis, though at times it may seem trifling and insignificant, is governed and controlled by the great scholastic doctrine which can be expressed in this way: It is through the realisation in history of the two *missions* of the Son and of the Spirit that we have access to an understanding of the divine life in its two *processions*. The unfathomable mystery of the fecundity and love of God is revealed to us by the two 'events' of the Incarnation of the Son and the sending of the Spirit. Thus the Church is the Body of Christ and the Communion of the Spirit. Unfortunately historians were right when they observed, from before the Council, that this doctrine of *missions* and *processions* had very little place in current teaching. It would seem that this was due to ignorance among the Latins of the theology of the eastern Fathers.

It is, then, by discerning the work of the Spirit that we can observe, in the present-day Church, the new awareness of the Trinitarian basis of the Church, as a means of spiritual renewal. In fact there is general agreement that there is among Christians a re-awakening of faith, in the Spirit, at the level of the actual life of the people of God, and not just at the higher level of sanctity. We will enumerate, though there will not be time to analyse them, the various points and places at which, today, we may discern the presence, unknown or recognised, of the Spirit.

(a) Celebration

Perhaps it is here that ordinary Christian people are most aware of the renewal of the Church, both in the Eucharistic celebration of established congregations and in the rapidly growing spontaneous prayer groups.

The starting point is the structural reform of the liturgy, which has been purged of its centuries-old routines in favour of an active understanding of the biblical readings, of the sacramental symbols, and of the dimensions of the mystery at its heart. But beyond this process of reform the liturgy is enlivened by community participation, which, while it does not detract from the rite, discreetly introduces spontaneous elements, in the way of spoken interpolations or external gestures. It would certainly not be arbitrary to ascribe these features, by which personal fervour is nurtured, to the Spirit, to the *impulse* of the Spirit. This accounts for the celebration's festive character—fervently desired, and occasionally achieved, though not without a degree of deritualisation, in a sober joy which astounds morose conformity. The new Churches in the Third World, where animism provides some very valuable elementary sensitivities, are clearly more lively than western Churches, which suffer from the coldness of Roman objectivity.

This enlivening process encourages the development of new forms of prayer, of rhythmic prayers, of appropriate songs, of textual changes. It was given impetus by an instruction issued by the Congregation on Liturgy: 'If there is to be a full renewal of liturgy, we cannot be satisfied with texts translated from other languages. New original creations will be necessary.'[2]

The major sacraments are rediscovering a structural dimension which has been for long atrophied in the West, through the rôle given to the Spirit, particularly in the Eucharist, where close doctrinal attention is again being paid to the epiclesis. This is why a good number of celebrants prefer the three new prayers of consecration to the first one, which had no explicit epiclesis. We should note, however, that, to the great regret of pastors and catechists, confirmation has not yet acquired its full significance either in doctrine or in celebration.

(b) Testimony

In a very different field, that of the transmission of the faith, there is, correspondingly, a very noticeable shift of emphasis and tone. Pride of place is no longer given to indoctrination, with its conceptualisations and abstractions; and testimony, with its character of subjective and contagious experience, has come to be more highly valued. Of course this idea comes from the purest evangelical tradition. But in reaction against the Lutheran doctrine of faith, and, more recently, against the modernist concept of assent, the word has been suspected of allowing too great a place to experience at the expense of dogmatic objectivity and the authority of the teaching office. The crisis is past, and both words find their way normally and effectively into the texts of the Council. Everywhere, in the directives on catechetical instruction, for adults as well as for children, and in the exhortations to dialogue with unbelievers, the most important place of all is given to testimony, while teaching is relegated to second place. Pope Paul VI expressed it vigorously in a declaration in which every word is significant: 'Today, more than ever, the Word of God can only be proclaimed and heard if it is accompanied by testimony to the power of the Holy Spirit, working in the activity of Christians in the service of their brothers, at those points at which their existence and their future are involved.'[3] And, after the synod of 1974, the apostolic exhortation in which Paul VI sums up the experiences of the bishops, not only stresses the pedagogical value of testimony but makes it the vital element in the transmission of faith. 'The whole Church must be bearing testimony', say the bishops of the Parisian region on their visit to Rome (September 1977), 'not as one who conveys the truth externally, but as one who participates in, discerns and reveals the meaning and profound significance of a positive experience of life.'

(c) Tradition and revelation

'Evangelisation must not be thought of as a transmission of truth, but as the incarnation of the gospel in contemporary historical reality.'[4] The intense effort of the pastoral office, in all the Churches and in most varied forms, clearly illustrates this principle, which now controls the life of the Church—without, however, undermining the teaching office. It is not simply a question of the improvement, to a greater or lesser degree, of recipes for the giving of instruction through catechesis and preaching; it is a question of restoring to the 'pastoral office' the rôle of motive force in the believing community of the Church itself and in the activation of revelatory tradition. Thus *doctrine* and *pastoral* activity are brought into positive correlation.

In fact, at this level, the pastoral office is the development of tradition in history, whose content is an essential part of Christian fact. For history is not simply a kind of stage setting which has no effect upon the characters in the play. If tradition is memory, and faithful memory, it is also presence, the place of synthesis between what is transmitted and present experience, brought about by the working of the Spirit. A deposit, but, as St Irenaeus says, 'a deposit that is always new, rejuvenating the vase of the expressions in which it is found'. It is as though Christ can be truly seen only in the light of the Resurrection with the help of all that is human down the ages. The ever more effective transfiguration of human reality thus becomes, somehow, a *condition* of the realisation of Christ, and it is the Spirit who unceasingly recalls him through the medium of the complex interplay of relations between men. Thus the era of the world is also the era of the Spirit.

Such is the *economy* in which the permanent articulation of the mission of the Son and the mission of the Spirit is the earthly expression of the 'processions' of Trinitarian being. We would like to think that the common insight which Christians have into the commitment demanded by their faith, brings them an implicit understanding of God—Father, Son and Spirit. Undoubtedly this is the great benefit that results from the introduction of historicity into the building up of the Church.

(d) Charisms

At the same time there is another element which, after a certain atrophy, is today recovering its rôle and its meaning: 'the community of Christians is not formed solely by individual sanctifying graces, but also by charisms—special graces by which the Spirit makes them fit and ready to undertake the various tasks and functions necessary for the renewal of the Church and its building up.'[5]

As Cardinal Suenens said to the Council at the beginning of discussion on this text, the Church has always been in the enjoyment of these social graces, which are of a different quality from the individual graces; but for structural reasons, and because of individualistic mentalities, these 'charisms' were considered as more or less extraordinary, and not very desirable for the general run of the faithful. In proportion as the collective consciousness of the 'people of God' sprang to life again, so the need grew for these gifts of the Spirit, not only for the more spectacular operations, but also for simpler, more widely-distributed ones. That is where the sense, so widespread today, of the co-responsibility of all in the building up of the Church has its roots. It is not the least of the re-awakenings brought about by the Spirit.

The typical characteristics of these charisms is that they are not, of themselves, 'instituted', or even inspired by the institution. They spring, so to speak, from the present situation and its pressures, from an event favourable to the Word of God. Thus they are doubly free, as the Christian discovers when, to his surprise and joy, he is seized by them, spontaneously, outside accepted frameworks and formulas. The 'prophet'—the most significant of the charisms—who speaks his message where it is appropriate, outside the established order, brings to his people a joyous certainty, not about doctrine in general, but about the concrete action to be performed, in an area in which the institution had no guidance to give. What was, for certain schools of spirituality, the discernment of spirits in individual life, is effected by the charism amid the confusions and shocks of collective events. Thus the Spirit builds up the Body of Christ in the fabric of history, which itself is constantly renewed. 'Being-in-the-world commits the Church to being more than simply an agent for the sacramentalisation of the established order. It makes of the Church a prophetic agent for the change and transformation which will bring peace and justice among men.'[6]

3. SCRIPTURE BECOMES WORD

Sic Deus, qui olim locutus est, sine intermissione cum dilecti Filii sui sponsa colloquitur,—et Spiritus Sanctus, per quem viva vox Evangelii in Ecclesia, et per ipsam in mundo resonat, credentes in omnem veritatem inducit, verbumque Christi in eis abundanter inhabitare facit. Instead of translating this text of the Council,[7] we quote from a text by the group which evidently prepared it, in the Report of the Secretariat for Unity: 'The Word of God is not simply a source of definable truths. . . . The Word of God, made present and contemporary in different ways in the Church and by the Church, is also a means appointed by God in his *economy* for making his salvation available to us. By his Word Christ is present for us, and he communicates grace to us.' *Economy* is precisely the concept which expresses the unique and varied rôle of the Father, the Son and the Holy Spirit in making the Word *present and contemporary*.

God speaks today. We find an understanding of the Word of God where it is at work in the world, in the community. The life of the Church *enters into* the text and vitalises it. The aim is not to apply the ideas of the gospels to the problems of today, but to read the Word of God in the history of today. St Francis of Assisi and St Dominic, in their prophetic reading of the gospel in the thirteenth century, reactivated, at a particular point in time and in close relationship with the history of their time, the unique proclamation of Good News to the poor. At the end of this twentieth century 'we must translate the parable of the Rich Man and Lazarus in economic and political terms, in terms of human rights, of relationships between the first, second and third worlds'.[8] 'Thou shalt love thy neighbour': today the Samaritan reaches out, in the long term, across structures and frontiers to 5,000 million neighbours. The literal exegesis of the text is no more than a support for a hermeneutic extending throughout time and space. Here, for example, are prophets of the Messianic Age rising up for the peoples of Latin America, announcing the Gospel of Liberation. And so on. Scripture becomes Word. We are not a little surprised to read in Origen[9] this statement, which seems modernist: '*Haec Scriptura, quae prius in* litteris *erat, modo, in Ecclesia Christi, revelante Domino,* loquela *effecta est.*'

Of course the written text of the Bible is the necessary and irreplaceable vehicle of the Word, as it is its radical standard of reference, both in understanding and in institution. It has sometimes happened in the Church, and precisely in 'prophetic' times, that people have surrendered to an understanding of the present which has implicitly rejected any continuity between the work of Christ and that of the Spirit, and which has led them off into flights of fancy which have taken no account of historical reality. It remains true that actual involvement in events brings about, by the presence of the Spirit, a deeper understanding of the faith, which owes more to contemplative experience than to speculative theology or dogmatic development. Revelation attains its fullness, its meaning, its reality, in the faith which receives it. 'Events constitute a salvation history which is already significant in itself. But they disclose their full meaning as a manifestation of God's plan only if they come to reality in the consciousness of the people of God. It must be clearly understood that revelation cannot happen in history unless it happens at the same time in the faith of the people of God. In other words, there is no revelation in the sense of a content of truth of transcendent origin, unless there is an interiorisation of this revelation in human consciousness. Revelation indicates, inseparably, the action of God in history and the believing experience of the people of God, which is translated into an interpretative expression of that action. Thus the faith-response of the people of God belongs to the actual content of what is the Word of God for us.'[10]

In fact, at the present time, in the Church in evolution, at this meeting point of structural reform and spiritual renewal, we are witnessing a shift in the interpretation of Scripture. Well before the Council we were acquainted with the multiplication of biblical groups, whether in isolation or within the framework of the movements of Catholic Action, whose chief concern was commentary on a text by a competent exegete, who thus led and controlled the thinking of the participants with professional and ecclesiastical authority. This was the beneficial result of biblical studies, which, after the modernist crisis, had regained scope and influence in the Catholic Church, and freed catechesis from its abstract formalism. In this context, the Word of God was understood objectively, in a relatively informed way, and the subjective expression of faith played only a secondary rôle. But thereafter, in several Churches—in Italy, in France, in Spain, and even more in the new Christian communities in Africa and Latin America—little 'basic communities' as they are called (80,000 in Brazil) proliferated. In these groups the main concern was no longer instruction in objective truth, but a sharing of faith-experiences, carried out at the places where believers confronted everyday realities, in their varied human contexts and with their political implications, with the object of finding there, in the light of the gospel, the action of God, the presence of the Spirit. Clearly it is not a matter of defining or affirming articles of faith, of reaching conclusions, nor for that matter of exercises in casuistry, but of interpreting the aspirations, needs and trials of men through the discernment of 'signs of the times'. These 'basic communities'—whose popular spontaneity distinguishes them sharply from the 'aristocratism' of the biblical groups—are ideal places for a re-reading of the Word of God, for a renovation of the language of faith, in the place where, as the world is built, the kingdom of God is built too, from the base upwards. Thus the incorporation in Christ of all human reality and the work of the Spirit, 'who renews the face of the earth', are brought together in a concrete way, in the midst of events. The realism of the Incarnation operates, in action, within the realism of Creation. After what we have said, it is possible to discern here a practical understanding, implicit yet penetrating, of the double mission of the Son and the Spirit.

4. GOD THE UNKNOWN

In the light of this new spirituality, we can get a perspective on the numerous works which are published—both learned and popular—on God, on our conceptions of God, on our language (the most ordinary as well as the most learned): Can we name God? Can we 'unmask' God? We would be wrong, I think, to see in these questionings only an affirmation of atheism. Most often, the God who is subjected to this lively criticism (which even goes so far as to announce his cultural 'death') is not the God of Jesus Christ but the God of deism, part of the heritage of the degenerate metaphysics of the philosophy of the Enlightenment.

The God in question is a rational God, the end term in a progression of casualty, a God located in a world which is foreign to our own. Almighty arbiter of human destiny, guarantor of the established order, by a providence which operates through earthly powers, a God who is unmovable and impassible in his eternity, in no way involved in the history of men, who attach to him the unbearable mystery of their hopes and their sufferings. A popular conception of the 'Good God', supported by the summary 'proofs' supplied by the Greek philosophers of pure Act (Aristotle) and supreme Idea (Plato). Nietzsche, who knew what he was talking about, rightly described all this as Platonism for the people.

This deism dominated the thought and devotion of the last two centuries to a much greater degree than is commonly supposed. It has been said that Christianity had more deists than Christians. This popular religion of the Absolute culminated in a personal and social 'alienation'. In the nineteenth century, in a 'bourgeois' society, catechesis and preaching were infected with it; and theological teaching was dominated on the one hand by the treatise *De Deo Uno*, without reference to Scripture, and on the other hand by a metaphysical Christology, without reference to the history of God. And now, in spite of a few aberrations, we are rediscovering the God of Jesus Christ, and as we do so, and confess the Father, we find meaning again in the mystic theme of the 'unknownness' of God, disclosed by the Son, Jesus Christ, the man among men, who can in no way be regarded as guarantor of the established order.

The 'mystery', in a situation of fulfilment—in time (God speaks today) and in space (the Word of God is in the world)—is thus open to the communion of men. God has come out of himself, and—a scandal to the gentiles—has emptied himself in order to be truly man, universal man. The Trinitarian revelation, completed in the work of the Spirit who determines history, is the foundation of the Church, its first structural principle.

'The grace of our Lord *Jesus Christ*, the love of God the *Father*, the communion of the *Spirit*, be always with you': it is with keen awareness that the Christian today hears this prayer of welcome to the Eucharistic gathering.

Translated by G. W. S. Knowles

Notes

1. 94th General Congregation.
2. On 25 January 1969.
3. Letter to Cardinal Roy (1971).
4. National Conference of the Italian Church, Rome, 30 October 1976.
5. Constitution *Lumen Gentium*, § 12.
6. Mgr Reus-Jroylan, Bishop of Puerto Rico, in his Pastoral Letter of 19 November 1970.
7. Constitution on Revelation, § 8.
8. John-Paul II, speech at UNO, 2 October 1979.
9. *In Jesu Nave*, hom. 20, 5.
10. Fr Geffré, in an article entitled, significantly, 'Le déplacement actuel de l'herméneutique' in *Mélanges Castelli* (Padua 1980) 44.

Giuseppe Ruggieri

The Rediscovery of the Church as an Evangelical Brotherhood

THE TERM brotherhood or fraternity is loaded with Utopian and sectarian connotations. In his 'testament' Sartre sees the 'fraternity' dreamed of by the leaders of the French Revolution, as a delicate point still awaiting a response from history.[1] In fact it is a word which inspires a new quality of life alike in modern western youth and peoples oppressed by military dictatorships or by economic dependence on the rich countries, even to the point of pain and death. The word has a fascination from which it is impossible to escape, even though historically it has been bound up with Utopianism and sectarianism, especially in Christian countries.

1. THE LANGUAGE OF THE COUNCIL

The use of the word 'brotherhood' or 'fraternity' in the texts of Vatican II is not univocal. It occurs 26 times: 12 in *Gaudium et Spes*, 4 in *Lumen Gentium*, 4 in *Presbyterorum Ordinis*, 2 in *Apostolicum Actuositatem* and once in *Ad Gentes*, *Orientalium Ecclesiarum*, *Perfectae Caritatis*, *Unitatis Redintegratio*. Sometimes the word 'brotherhood' is used to indicate the Church gathered round the Eucharist (LG § 26) or the community as such (LG § 28, PO § 6); or it refers to the nature of the bond that unites Christians to each other: *caritas fraternitatis* (fraternal love) (PO § 9, AA § 23); in OE § 30 'brotherly love' is the link that should exist between eastern and western Christians; UR § 7 says that the brotherhood that exists between separated Christians is the fruit of each one's union with the Trinity; the most restricted usage is the designation of fraternity as the particular relationship existing between priests (LG § 28; PO § 28: twice in the same paragraph) or between those belonging to the same religious congregation (PC § 15); LG § 41 speaks of the family as a *fraternitas caritatis*.

In 14 other places (all 12 in *Gaudium et Spes*, in AA § 14 and AG § 8) fraternity is used to designate the ideal of human life together as such, without any ecclesiastical specification.

The most illuminating texts are those in which the Church is said to be a sign of brotherhood which enables people to talk to each other (dialogue to take place between men) (GS 92) or that the gospel has always been a leaven of brotherhood (AG § 8) or that Christians' action in the world should transform that feeling for the need of solidarity which is a sign of our time into a sincere and authentic 'feeling of brotherhood' (AA § 14).

An analysis of the texts in which Vatican II uses the term 'brother' leads to analogous results. The word 'brother' is used 108 times (26 in UR, 20 in LG, 17 in GS, 14 in PO, 11 in AA, 6 in AG, 5 in PC, 3 in OE, 1 in DV, SC, CD, OT, NA, GE). It is never used in its primary natural sense but always as a religious term in the salvation history sense (Christ as our brother or first born among brothers, recognising Christ in our brothers, Christians as brothers, priests as brothers, separated brethren, our brothers who have died, our brothers in glory, the members of the same religious congregation as brothers, all men as brothers). Only once, referring to Acts 1:14, the 'brothers of Jesus' are mentioned (LG § 59). It is also interesting to note how in *Gaudium et Spes* the meaning of universal brotherhood prevails (5 times out of 17), in *Lumen Gentium* the Christological meaning (5 times out of 20) and the intra-ecclesial (6 times out of 20), in *Unitatis Redintegratio*, the ecumenical meaning of separated brethren (24 times out of 24!) and in *Presbyterorum Ordinis* the 'clerical' (8 times out of 14).

These brief data suggest a conclusion: in the Council texts that speak of the Church as brotherhood there is a tension. On the one hand brotherhood is presented as the important thing about the Church to which everything else must be referred. Even the document with the greatest 'clerical' preoccupation, which stresses the peculiar brotherhood of priests, does not fail to relate this to the more fundamental and traditional brotherhood of all Christians (PO § 9: like other Christians, priests are disciples of the Lord; having been reborn in baptism they are brothers among brothers).[2] This gives us the fundamental ecclesiological inspiration of the Council as substantially egalitarian and striving to restore the primacy of communion and what unites rather than what divides.[3]

But the other side is even more significant. It is not the eccclesial brotherhood that is not the prime analogate, but the ideal of universal brotherhood for which ecclesial brotherhood is a sign (GS § 92, AG § 8). The original fact, on which both ecclesial and human universal brotherhood depend is the event of Christ.

The use of the word brotherhood in the Council texts avoids the tendency of ecclesiomonism. The Church is a reality signifying something which does not take its origin in itself but in Christ; it does not find its fulfilment in itself but in all humanity, in the ideal of brotherhood and solidarity which runs through history and gives it life.

2. THE WEIGHT OF MEMORY

Terminology is one thing, history as it actually occurs is another. The Council language is like one of those fertile moments in human and ecclesial becoming, which it is then up to history to make grow. This means that the Council language must be confronted with the language of the past and of the present to make clear both what it is trying to say and its possible developments.

It must assume the weight of the Church's memory and make the effort to welcome in the present all the wealth revealed in Christ's gospel.

Firstly, in order to show the 'novelty' of the Council language, it is worth comparing it with the dominant attitudes in the Church on the eve of Vatican I.

In an essay which gives an excellent *status quaestionis* on this, J. Ratzinger lamented 'the mistaken individualism from which Christianity suffers because it has abandoned the term brother and the attitude that goes with it'.[4]

The mistake arose from a serious ecclesial imbalance which maintained that the true essence of the Church reposed primarily in the monastic order or the clerical condition, and only in a derived manner was it participated in by ordinary Christians. The *Glossarium ad scriptores mediae et infimae latinitatis* by Charles Du Cange gives eight different uses of the word *fraternatis*. Of these five are specifically ecclesial. Among these only one is referred to the whole Church as such. Otherwise monastic fraternity is the primary analogy: 'a group of brothers, that is to say monks'; 'closely linked society between monks of different monasteries, in which they share each other's goods to the point that they are considered to be brothers of the other monastery. . .'; 'gifts offered to monasteries by those who have accepted their fraternity'; 'brotherhood is the name given to laity who are admitted to share in the prayers and benefits of the monks'. This mistake is ancient, it goes back to the patristic age. St John Chrysostom tries to combat it and states clearly that in the New Testament the term 'brother' refers not to the monk but to the Christian.[5] But Cassian contrasted the *fratres* (monks) with the other Christians who are called *seculares*. Augustine generally remains faithful to primitive usage and calls Christians brothers but he sometimes uses the term to refer only to monks.[6]

The notion of brotherhood in the New Testament is quite different. Even in the Qumran writings (especially the 'Damascus Document') there is an attempt to overcome the conception of brotherhood as a sect, as a group separated from the rest of the people.[7] Jesus not only went beyond this radically sectarian limit but presupposed a conception of man and God which made it an impossibility. In his preaching the true enemy is no longer another man but the egoistic self ('his own life': Luke 14:26). We are obliged to be totally available to others. Then Jesus' idea of God the Father is radically different; we must love our enemies because they are sons of the Father who makes rain fall on the just and the unjust (Matt. 5:44-45).[8] The new concept of brotherhood in Christianity derives from the new relationship with God: 'Who is my mother and who are my brothers? . . . Whoever does the will of God is my brother, sister and mother.' The difference has been rightly pointed out between the Christian idea of brotherhood and the 'naturalist' universalism of Stoic brotherhood.[9] Christian brotherhood is not a given fact but a duty, a possible condition for those who have found the right relationship with the Father. It is a historical task and not the purely verbal 'eyewash' of an ideology.

And it is this same radical nature of the concept of God which imposes the duty of egalitarian brotherhood on the community of the disciples. Even the text of Matthew giving them their mission must not break the rule given in Matt. 23:8. This remains the criterion by which to judge any temptations to grasp power in the community: 'But you are not to be called rabbi, for you have one teacher and you are all brethren.' The conciliar translation of this gospel precept is given in LG § 32: 'Although through the will of God some are appointed teachers and dispensers of mysteries and pastors for the others, yet there is true equality in dignity between them (*aequalitas quoad dignitatem*) and in common action by all the faithful in the building up of the body of Christ.'

Evangelical brotherhood does not exclude differences in intensity. The language of Jesus himself varies and the peculiar brotherhood of the disciples is recognised. But because of the new conception of God this special brotherhood remains within a human context which does not admit separation. (Thus in Matt. 25:31-46 and Luke 10:25-37 the criterion of brotherhood is radically extra-ecclesial and exists because of human need.)[10] It cannot be absorbed into sectarianism.

Thus the equilibrium of gospel brotherhood is particularly delicate. Even within the Church it is easy to forget the one Father and the radical brotherhood of all, so that specific functions become dominative. Matt. 23:8-11 warns against this risk. And there is also the risk that the community will fail to regard outsiders with the eyes of the Father who makes the rain fall on the just and the unjust. Non-Christians may be regarded merely as 'outsiders' (1 Thes. 4:12; 1 Cor. 5:12-13; Col. 4:5).

The brotherhood (synonymous with 'Church' in 1 Pet. 2:17; 5:9) must guard against this danger. And it must remember that the most radical distinction is not between outside and inside the Church but between the 'outer man' who is exposed to corruption and the 'inner man', who is within every believer (2 Cor. 4:16). The true separation is not, as Augustine will explain later in *De Civitate Dei*, between those who belong and those who do not belong to the visible community; it is more radical and in the last analysis it is an eschatological event (as the parables of the weeds, Matt. 13:36-43, and of the net and the fishes, Matt. 13:47-50 show).

And above all the community must remember that the sacrifice which redeemed the people took place 'outside' and so they must go outside all ritual observance to follow Christ (Heb. 13:12-13).

And the new community of brothers, made up of those who were once far off and those who were near, Jews and gentiles, must try to do something about the Jewish 'brothers' who remain outside (Rom. 9:3), because there may be a 'hostility' to the preaching of the gospel; but this 'hostility' does not nullify the even greater love expressed in their 'election' because 'the gifts and the call of God are irrevocable' (Rom. 11:28-9). Here too we have the Christian notion of God who does not allow the brotherhood to be reduced to 'Church' or 'sect' but opens it up towards the limitless horizons offered by the God of Jesus Christ.

3. BROTHERHOOD AS ADORATION

The idea of brotherhood as the quality of life of the Church is sometimes trivialised by the accusation that it is an attempt to adapt to the democratic spirit and thus confuses the Christian spirit with the spirit of the world. This accusation is clearly absurd, as can be shown from the simple fact that the early churches, which existed in a much more authoritarian world than the present one, practised forms of 'democracy' (for example, the election of bishops) which are far removed from its present practice.

Thus brotherhood in the Church is something quite different from an uncritical adaptation to the ways of the world. It is founded on the concept of God which was the basis of the teaching and practice of Jesus of Nazareth. Thus the choice between a Church which is a brotherhood and a hierarchical Church, in which there are superiors and subordinates, is in the last analysis the choice between a concept of God based on the Christian gospel and a religious and social idea derived from other sources. This is clearly expressed in Luke 22:24-30: there is a radical difference between the 'gentiles' and the community of the disciples. Among the 'gentiles' those in authority rule over them, in the community of disciples authority means service.[11]

The God who is the basis of the preaching and practice of Jesus of Nazareth is described in the action of him who sits at table and serves his brothers. The eschatological return of the 'master' (the Son of Man) is described as girding himself and serving at table (Luke 12:37).

The New Testament developed this concept of God by deepening its Trinitarian root: God is communion. The Father has given everything to the Son and the gift is the very life of God. This is why the Spirit, who is the divine self-giving, leads to the truth, the revelation of the depths of God. The Church worked hard to understand the radical difference of the mystery with which it had been entrusted. In fact it was only slowly, after the third century, that it overcame the 'subordinationist' principle, which introduced subordination within the Trinitarian communion and derived from a misunderstanding of the divine 'monarchy', the 'unity of the principle' which does not arise in God from inferiority. The Son's obedience (and thus all Christian obedience) is 'receiving himself' (only possible in the freedom of communion and giving) and not

C

'submitting himself'. And because it is 'receiving himself' it is radical and not just a purely external act. 'Receiving' escapes the logic of domination and submission and becomes life in common and 'gift'.

A Church which introduces subordinations within itself shows that it has not understood the depths of the mystery. Of course, because it is a reality which is not yet totally transfigured but subject to the contradictions of sin and division, it cannot escape the necessity for disciplinary regulations and laws. Paul himself, a strenuous defender of Christian freedom, does not fail to resolve certain conflicts by his authority 'but not to command your faith' (2 Cor. 1:24). Thus the style of radical brotherhood is not a simple fact of the Christian community. It is possible only as the practice of adoration, as the recognition of the transcendence of the Trinitarian communion, in which we are all called to share. And this does not mean there will not be quarrels, even bitter ones, within the community, as we see from the example of Peter and Paul in the early Church (with accusations of guilt and insincerity: Gal. 2:11 ff). But in adoration all differences are overcome by the awareness of a communion which has been given as a fact that is even greater than division and dispute. Therefore 'all the faithful should remember that the better they promote, and thus live, the union of Christians, the more they try to live a life in accordance with the gospel. Thus the more closely they are united in communion with the Father, the Word and the Holy Spirit, the more they will be able to grow in mutual brotherhood' (between separated Christians: UR § 7). The communion of God is not greedy possession, even of the Son which is why he was able to 'empty himself' to become like us. Brotherhood is only possible as a result of this adoring adhesion to the mystery of the Father, the Son and the Spirit.

So: resistance to radical brotherhood in the structuring of the Church, a brotherhood in which there is 'equality of dignity' in which inevitable differences are experienced in the awareness of a greater communion given to us is resistance to the God of Jesus Christ. This means that the attempts to restore the style of brotherhood and communion to the structures of the Church (effective synodality and conciliarity, decentralisation and the restoration of the sense of responsibility in the individual churches, the overcoming of the deadening dichotomy between clergy and laity, etc.) are not merely fashionable democratisation. They reveal the Christian faith which has experienced God's terrible sweetness, which has come close to us because in him there is no distance but only the immediate presence of giving.

4. BROTHERHOOD AS COMPANY

Medieval Latin has a term which expresses the experience of conviviality and the common human destiny: *companio*, someone who shares bread.[12]

Christians are brothers because they break bread together. This is a convivial act but upon it lies the judgment of the cross. This means that if anyone breaks bread together and excludes the weaker and the poorer from their table, what he or she is doing is 'not eating the Lord's supper' (1 Cor. 11:20). The brotherhood of the Church is either a radical 'company', the breaking of bread together with everyone else without taking any notice of religious barriers or social or cultural differences, or it is merely sectarian—it is not a memorial of the action of Jesus who sat down to table with publicans and sinners and who took upon himself the shame when he was crucified 'outside' the city.

Christian brotherhood imitates and re-enacts the Christological event every time it overcomes a barrier and has the courage to sit in company with the lowest. This is what distinguishes it from being merely a comforting group or 'in' group, or a moralist identification between the 'good', and the 'pious', and from every juvenile way of being together.

The sense of the Christological event as it has been passed down from New

Testament memory is not a generic and neutral manifestation of divine love for men. The special nature of the event of Jesus Christ is to be found in the parables of the lost sheep, the prodigal son and Jesus' own daily living, not just with the disciples but with publicans and sinners. In Jesus Christ, God reaches those who are outside, those who are far off, those for whom the dominant culture and religiosity see no future.

In Jesus Christ God's love is eccentric, outside the calm secure centre of those who are 'like us', outside the warm centre of shared love. In the mystery of the *kenosis* and death God descends to the 'underworld', because that is where the good news is preached,[13] where God is very far away and 'absent'. And this is the scandal of the cross, which reveals what God is. In Jesus Christ, God reveals himself as the mystery capable of embracing all, because he goes out to seek that which 'is lost', that which is far away. This is why there is more rejoicing over one repentant sinner than ninety-nine just. This is why the gospel message of brotherhood can contain the teaching 'blessed are you poor' together with 'woe to you that are rich' (Luke 6:20, 24). The true centre, where we must stand in order to grasp the special nature of the God of Jesus Christ, is the poor, the rejected. And the semantic fluctuation of the biblical term 'poor', which cannot be reduced to a single meaning, must make us beware of making the 'poor' a 'category', and thus trying to justify social conflicts. The poor man is a person with whom we should break bread, in the last analysis he is not someone to 'help' but someone to be with, to be a companion of, to rejoice, struggle and suffer with. He is not a 'recipient' but a *companion*. In this company Christian brotherhood can discover the true character of a 'sign'. The poor man is a 'universal' subject (like the 'sinner', the 'little one', the 'defeated', the 'oppressed'). Only those who can join them and 'stay with them' can enter the breadth and depth and height of God who embraces all and wants nothing and no one to perish but that all should be saved. Only if Christian brotherhood stands with those to whom the 'enemy's' lies have brought death and hopelessness, can it manifest the truth of the love which proclaimed victory over death in Christ. Only here, among the 'least' and those who are 'outside', can the gospel be proclaimed in all its power of liberation.[14]

Ecclesial brotherhood cannot be reduced to a sense of belonging to a social body governed by the same rules of behaviour, sharing the same religious responses and culture. It must expand so that it can breathe with the rhythm of all history, welcome every approach to solidarity and transform it into a genuine feeling of brotherhood (*Apostolicam Actuositatem* § 14).

In order to do this, it must renounce the logic of power and possession. It can only be achieved by those who do not think of their own condition as a 'possession' but are prepared to empty themselves. This means that there is a connection between the two aspects of Christian brotherhood (brotherhood as alternative to the authoritarian logic of power within the Church and brotherhood as companionship with the 'least'). Only a poor and brotherly Church can proclaim the good news to the poor. And only thus can preaching the gospel be distinguished from any political programme and become a revelation and proclamation of the freedom to which Christ has freed us.

5. BROTHERHOOD AS *KAIROS*

The new image of God revealed in Jesus Christ requires that the Church should be a fraternity to announce the gospel to the poor. This means that the Church must be structured as a living together of brothers equal in dignity, sharing their goods and being companions with the least and the littlest on earth. But all this is also *kairos*, the right moment in which to discover the grace that has been given us and which the churches cannot betray.

Today they are facing a change which is the modern age itself. Even in 1453 in *De pace fidei* Nicholas of Cusa saw the big problem raised by the times to come. Christian faith, faced with the great religious and cultural oppositions to come in modern times, could not make itself 'part' even of a religion. It was called to bring peace by revealing to every religion and every people the truth of the desire that was in them. Even the great historical 'enemy' of Christianity, Islam, was welcomed with magnanimity and its hopes accorded sympathy. But in the West, faith became a reason for war and conquest. And in the West too, nations were forced to seek a basis for common life and brotherhood in something other than the churches. This was a 'human rights movement', a 'lay' culture (which had arisen by 'separation' from the churches). Fraternity, together with liberty and equality, was the slogan adopted by a search for a basis for living together, a common 'human nature' prescinding from every faith. However, this search for what was 'common' outside any faith turned out to be a great illusion. Western civilisation developed an 'abstract' human nature, which was functional for the anonymous dominion of capital, but which had no face, no name, no hands to clasp in friendship. In the name of this abstract essence the West has annihilated cultures, peoples and civilisations. Especially in Latin America but also to a lesser extent in Asia and Africa, the European model of human nature acted as a destructive force. Even the churches joined in this operation, and their mission, the proclamation of the gospel of the God of Jesus Christ was accompanied by a work of cultural enslavement to the western abstract model of humanity.

The Christian churches have felt uncomfortable about this co-operation. Las Casas defended the right to diversity in the human race, de Foucaul, more recently, was able to imagine a Christian presence which was a respected friend of the Koran. However, the co-operation with the destroyers lasted a long time, even though the western abstract human nature is today in ashes. In this devastation the Church is tempted to grab back what has been taken away from her, to reappropriate the 'common' human nature and proclaim itself the only historical institution able to teach the way to live together in harmony and to rediscover humanity in its true dignity. In fact the West still maintains the 'power' of man but not the 'dignity'. The Christian churches, and especially the Catholic Church, could profit from this loss in their historical vendetta and reassert their own power, religious dignity and prestige. But this attempt would involve a complete change of course from that inspired by the Council. In this case the Church would not be reforming itself in obedience to Christ who conquered and ruled from the cross, as a sign in poverty of the extraordinary richness of God, as a simple brotherhood of communion, as a humble spreading of Christian brotherhood. It would respond to the crises afflicting modern society as a structure which is able to guarantee and guide. This temptation is the temptation of authoritarianism, putting in parentheses the conciliar indications (*Lumen Gentium*) that the only appropriate style of presence for the Church is that of Christ the servant. And in this temptation lies the root of the new attempt in the Church to restore a *potestas in temporalibus* through the claim that the Church is the exclusive possessor of the final truth about humanity. However, the brotherhood preached by Christ seems to point in another direction. The task of the disciples was to manifest the radical difference of the God who annihilated himself and sat down to table with the lowest, to manifest the new brotherhood which can be attained by those who worship the God who makes rain fall on the just and the unjust, who was put to death by the powerful and revealed in this his strange omnipotence.

And this is precisely why the Church must experiment within itself, try out the new brotherhood of taking it in turns to serve one another at table, breaking bread with publicans and sinners.

But this does not mean that that which is 'common' can be stated in a more or less neutral doctrine of the common nature and destiny of man. Neither can it be maintained by re-proposing a compact organism which offers secure guarantees and answers to questions about the ultimate meaning of things.

What is common, the origin of brotherhood, can only be given value and tasted by simple witness to the gratuitous nature of the Father's love which requires humble welcome, humble sharing, joyful serving of each other at table.

Then the churches could emerge as 'teachers' in humanity, at the very moment when they renounced their claim to call themselves such. They could bear witness to their capacity to call all who want to proclaim God's peace, which was bought dearly by him who was abandoned by his brothers and in absolute loneliness came close to all, the thieves he was crucified with, the dwellers in the place where 'God is not': crucified for our sins, descended into hell.

Translated by Dinah Livingstone

Notes

1. See especially part 2 of the interview in *Le Nouvel Observateur* (17 March 1980) p. 53 ff.

2. From Justin (*Apologia* I 65) and Tertullian (*De Baptismo* 20.5.) onwards it has been traditional in the Church to connect Christian brotherhood and baptism as a new birth in which God becomes the Father and the Church the mother. From the event of baptism something indestructible arises, so that Optatus of Milevis can apply to the relations between Catholics and Donatists the text of Isa. 66.5 in the Septuagint translation '. . . to those that hate you and do not want to call themselves your brothers, you reply: you are our brothers' (quoted by J. Ratzinger in 'Fraternité *Dict. de Spiritualité* col. 1153. Furthermore, baptism, as the indestructible foundation of communion between Christians, even if they are separated, plays a critical part throughout the history of the Church in determining the criteria for belonging to the Church.

3. Although we should point out that this inspiration coexists with another, opposite one. See A. Acerbi *Due ecclesiologie. Ecclesiologie giuridica ed ecclesiologia di communione nella Lumen Gentium* (Bologna 1975).

4. See the article quoted in note 2, col. 1161.

5. *Ibid.* col. 1155.

6. Cf. Mohrmann, *Etudes sur le latin des chrétiens* II (Rome 1961) p. 336. A. von Harnack's view that the title brother disappeared gradually from Christianity from the end of the third century onwards is substantially exact, although it could be modified somewhat. See J. O'Callaghan 'Persistencia del trato de "hermano" entre los christianos del siglo V' in *Anal. Sacra Tarrac.* (1961) pp. 1-5.

7. See H. Braun *Spätjüdisch-häretischer und frühchristlicher Radikalismus. Jesus von Nazareth und die essenische Qumransekte* (Tübingen 1957) I pp. 127-130.

8. See the article by H. Braun, quoted in note 7, II pp. 83-99.

9. J. Ratzinger, in the article quoted in note 2, col. 1142.

10. On the 'ecclesiastical' interpretation of the view that sees the Christian missionaries as the 'little ones' whom the pagans should welcome, see recently G. Lohfink 'Universalismus und Exklusivität des Heils im Neuen Testament' in W. Kasper *Absolutheit des Christentums* (Quaestiones disputatae 79) pp. 63-82, esp. 79-82.

11. For a deeper study of this point in relation to the meaning of ecclesial ministries, see G. Ruggieri 'Ministers e ruoli sociali in Aa Vv *Ministers e ruoli sociali* (Turin 1978) pp. 7-19.

12. This sense of the term *companio* still remains in other languages besides Italian. See e.g., the German *Kumpan* and *Kumpanei*. For more on 'company', see G. Ruggieri 'La compagnia dela fede' *Linee di teologia fondamentale* (Turin 1980); *idem.* in I. Mancini-G. Ruggieri *Fede e cultura* (1979) I pp. 49-83.

13. On the descent into hell, see H. U. von Balthasar in *Mysterium salutis* 6.

14. Hence we can understand rightly the privilege given to the poor in the Church's thinking, esp. in Latin America. See recently, R Muñoz *Evangelio y liberacion en America Latina. La teologia pastoral de Puebla* (Santiago 1980) pp. 25-38.

Joseph Komonchak

The Church Universal as the Communion of Local Churches

IT WAS explained to me by Professor Alberigo that my essay should illustrate 'how the integration and the tension between the local Churches and the universal Church constitute one of the permanent aspects of the theological structure of the Church'. We may begin by considering two ways of understanding these relationships.

The first may be called a 'descending' vision, an ecclesiology 'from above'. Here the relationship between the universal Church and the local Churches is that of a whole to its parts. Philosophically, the whole is conceived as a *totum potestativum* in which lower realities participate in the nature possessed in full by some prior and superior reality.[1] Organisationally, all authority resides in a central organ or bureau from which it is distributed out into field-offices, as in a modern transnational corporation. Theologically, this view is associated with what is sometimes called a 'Christo-monist' view of the Church, according to which the Risen Christ's authority in heaven and on earth is shared in first and fully by Peter (or the Pope) and is then distributed by him to others (apostles or bishops), by whom it is in turn distributed among others (priests and deacons). Quite often this view leads to an identification of the universal Church with the Church of Rome, so that the relationship between Church universal and local Churches becomes the relationship between that Church and the other Churches, almost as if the Church of Rome were not itself a local Church.

On the second, 'ascending' view, the whole is not conceived prior to the parts; rather the one whole comes to be, is constituted by, in, and out of the realisations of its many constituents. *All* the intrinsic and distinctive elements that constitute the reality are realised individually, and the relationships that make the individual realisations a single whole are grounded in a common participation in one reality constitutive of them all. Philosophically, the relationships are mutual mediations and the whole is co-constituted. Organisationally, the various bonds among the individual realisations, including the central and unifying authority, derive from, express, and serve the common and prior participation in a single reality. Theologically, this view is associated with a pneumatological or Trinitarian view of the Church, according to which each local self-realisation manifests the full spiritual reality of communion in Christ's Holy Spirit. On this second view, the question proposed for this essay can sound a little odd, for the 'universal Church' is not a reality separate from the 'local Churches'; the Church universal *is* the communion of the local Churches.

It is only a slight exaggeration to say that the movement of ecclesiology in this century has been from the first view to the second. Ideal-typically, Vatican I may be said to illustrate the first view and Vatican II the second. Historically, the first view guided a movement of Roman centralisation that is now over a thousand years long. Vatican II represented the first and still nascent effort to recall and to restore the theoretical and practical superiority of the second view, which had also prevailed in the ecclesiology of the first millennium.[2]

Again ideal-typically, defenders of the first view usually espouse a 'society-model' of the Church and the proponents of the second a 'communion-model'. The issue, however, is not whether the Church is either a society or a communion, but rather which of these notions is to prevail in a theology of the Church and in an appropriate Church polity. Put differently, the question is whether formal questions about the distribution of authority are to prevail over material questions about the nature of the common reality which constitutes the social body in which authority has its place and is distributed. This question so dominated the conciliar discussions in which *Lumen Gentium* was elaborated that without a knowledge of it both the achievements and the weaknesses of that document are unintelligible.[3] In *Lumen Gentium*, the discussions of authority (ch. 3) follow the discussions of the spiritual reality of the Church as Mystery and as the people of God (chs. 1-2). But no real integration of the two discussions was possible, and the third chapter had to contain so many qualifications as to postpone to an uncertain future an adequate resolution of many theological and practical difficulties. Many elements of post-conciliar developments in the Catholic Church can be interpreted as the continuation of the debates the Council did not resolve.

In the following pages, I will outline a theological interpretation and defence of an ecclesiology of the universal Church that begins with the local Church (an ecclesiology 'from below') and then indicate some of the difficulties that lie in the way of a practical realisation of this view in the Roman Catholic Church today.

Chapters 1 and 2 of *Lumen Gentium* can be understood as extended explications of what is summarily stated when the Church is called a 'community of faith, hope, and love' (LG § 8) or 'a communion of life, love and truth' (LG § 9). Although obviously in need of specification in terms of the biblical, traditional, liturgical and theological images and statements that abound in those chapters, the two phrases have the advantage of offering summary formulas that can orient a discussion. As in *Lumen Gentium* itself, in what follows is not forgotten that this community or communion is a visible social reality; what is at stake, however, is what that visible social reality is.

To say that the Church is a 'community' or 'communion' is to say that the Church is an achievement of common meaning and value.[4] In the Council's formulas, this common meaning and value which constitute and distinguish the Church are the faith, hope and love by which Christians together receive the redemptive Word of God and, looking forward to the future of his promise, live out the loving service of God and neighbour. Everything else in the Church is in the service of this central, constitutive reality without which something other than the Church of God is being realised.

The social reality so realised is at once the *Ecclesia de Trinitate*—People of God, Body of Christ, Temple of the Holy Spirit—and the *Ecclesia de hominibus*. The splendid biblical, traditional, liturgical images, symbols and statements are by the grace of God true of a quite human community and are realised in quite concrete sets of experiences, understandings, judgments, statements, decisions, actions, relationships, structures, etc. These sets of activities, which can also be studied by the social scientists, are part of the theological 'ontology' of the Church.[5] 'The creation of the Spirit' is achieved in and through various quite human forms and patterns of social relationship.

If these forms and patterns by which the Church realises itself are not attended to, concretely described, and understood, ecclesiologists will run the danger of conceiving the Church (to paraphrase Marx's critique of Feuerbach) as an abstract being outside the world. But if attention is given to the created subjects and constituents of the Church's self-realisation, the Church will be understood as a group of human subjects engaged in a common task of self-realisation. The Church is not itself the divine initiative in Word and grace, but the free human response created by that Word and grace. As such, it is always first of all a concrete reality, *this* group of men and women, at *this* time and in *this* place, within *this* culture, responding to the Word and grace by which God gathers them into Christ. Furthermore, it is not an abstract Word that is preached and accepted in faith, but a Word that illumines a particular situation, responds to particular questions, and is expressed in particular languages, symbols, gestures, rites, etc. Redemptive grace is always concrete, an overcoming of particular instances of sin, a liberation from particular bonds and addictions. The Church that comes to be through faith, hope and love is not a realm beyond culture, history and society, but a concrete manifestation in human communities of particular places, times and cultures of the one transcendent and redemptive grace of God. In Hervé Legrand's words, the particular Church is 'the response to a gospel heard in a human space [culture] in its own language'.[6]

But if, as Legrand remarks, the Church 'was born universal' at Pentecost, it is not contradictory but only paradoxical to say that 'the universality of the Church is always a concrete universality which only exists through its particularity'.[7] There is no universal Church except in and through the self-realisations of local Churches. The Church universal *is* 'God's beloved in Rome', 'the Church of God which is at Corinth', 'the Churches of Asia', 'the Churches of Galatia', 'the saints in Christ Jesus who are at Philippi', 'the saints and faithful brethren in Christ at Colossae', 'the Church of the Thessalonians', and all the other Churches established everywhere since the days of the apostles. This is not to say that the universal Church is only the collection or sum-total of all particular Churches; for what makes a group of men and women the Church in one place is what makes another group the Church in another place: one communion of life, love and truth is realised everywhere through the one Word, the one baptism, the one Eucharist, the one Spirit, under the one God and Father of all. It is this communion which permits a Catholic to discover 'a brotherhood of common response' not only across the centuries[8] but also across cultures. As Augustine was no less Catholic for being so clearly a fifth-century African, so also particular Churches are today no less Catholic for being clearly African, Asian, European, Latin American, etc. Nothing could be more fatal to an adequate ecclesiology than to counterpose unity and universality, particularity and catholicity.

The rise of ecclesiology to the status of a central theological discipline in the last century and a half can be read as part of the movement by which the Church has become increasingly aware of itself as 'a process of self-constitution, a *Selbstvollzug*'.[9] The Church has always been such a process, but in this historically conscious age it has become more and more conscious of this self-constituting activity. But this existential awareness of its historical self-project makes the question of its guiding principles all the more urgent. At Vatican I it was the rôle of the pope in that self-realisation of the universal Church that was most strongly and almost exclusively stressed; at Vatican II, his rôle has been placed in a more adequate ecclesiological context by the emphasis placed upon the activities and ministries, particularly those of the bishop, by which the local Churches realise themselves and thus the universal Church.

The Council itself, however, did not provide a full statement of a theology of the local Church,[10] and, in its discussions of a ministry to the universal Church, it did little more that juxtapose assertions about the College of Bishops to Vatican I's assertions about the papal primacy.[11] Great concern was evident lest the vindication of episcopal collegiality be considered to imply limits upon the sovereignty of the pope. Similarly, the relations between the College of Bishops and the individual local bishop were also described in deliberately open terms. Because the Council abstained from settling many disputed points, the controversy between an 'ascending' and a 'descending' view of the Church is still being carried on both in theory and in practice. It will be helpful at least briefly to take note of some of the features of this post-conciliar struggle.

There is, first of all, the simple fact that the Catholic Church as it exists today is the product of centuries of development. History, too, has its laws of inertia, and a centralising movement with a thousand years behind it is not likely to be significantly redirected much less reversed in a mere fifteen years. Not only have patterns of relationship and dependence become habitual and assumed the status of the taken-for-granted, but an elaborate theory has been constructed, particularly over the last century, to legitimate them. If it can be argued that this 'descending' theory is inadequate to the ecclesial realities as lived out in the first millennium of the Church's life and as recovered in the teaching of Vatican II, it is foolish to deny that it still has its adherents and that it appears still to prevail in many Roman circles.

Some indications of the continued power of this view are visible in the discussions among the *coetus* responsible for composing the new Code of Canon Law. A canon proposed for Book II, *De Populo Dei*, asserts the duty of the faithful to remain in communion with the universal Church and to fulfil their duties towards both the universal and the particular Church. One bishop proposed that the particular Church be mentioned first on the grounds that 'insertion into the universal Church takes place through the particular Church'. The Relator refused the suggestion because, he said, 'Christ founded the Church as a universal unity'.[12] In the discussions on the *Lex Ecclesiae Fundamentalis*, earlier affirmations of the collegial significance of the Synod of Bishops have been dropped, so that this body now appears simply as a body assistant to the pope, on the same level as the College of Cardinals.[13] Some consultors regard Episcopal Conferences as operating *ex delegatione Summi Pontificis*.[14] A suggestion to add to the strong assertion of the universal ordinary supreme authority of the pope a statement affirming that this power is limited by 'the power of bishops which is also a power of divine right' was refused on the grounds that the pope can always exercise his authority.[15] That freedom is also asserted when a canon states that the pope always acts in communion with other bishops but need not act collegially[16] and when in several canons the possibility of the College of Bishops initiating collegial activities is seriously compromised.[17] The cumulative effect of these decisions is to concentrate the *sollicitudo omnium ecclesiarum* in the hands of the pope.

A second element in contemporary tensions derives from what sociologists call 'ethnocentrism'. This can take many forms: the assumption of the superiority of one's own culture ('civilisation'), a classicistic, normative notion of culture, nostalgia for former and simpler times, a naïve belief in the 'march of progress', etc. When any of these prevails, there is a tendency to identify the Church with particular cultural realities and to ignore or overlook the differences between what is Christian and what is merely a cultural variable. The latter distinction, however, is only easy in theory and upon reflection, as for example when the 'essence' of the Church is distinguished from its 'forms'. How difficult in practice it is to make this distinction anyone can note who has tried to distinguish the two in himself or in his own 'form' of the Church. It is no easy task to describe the Church as a reality prior to any particular self-realisation. The difficulties that result affect all the Churches, at least in the form of a temptation, whether in the central circles of Rome, in the ancient Churches, or in the 'young' Churches. If today many of the tensions are experienced in the efforts of the Churches in, say, Africa or Asia to clear the ground for an indigenous realisation of the Church, they may be expected to become even more acute when particular Churches become ever more effectively the subjects of their own self-realisations. Ethnocentrism is not only a

Eurocentrist temptation. One must expect a long period of 'negotiation' of the legitimate differences and essential common elements.

For example, at the 1980 Synod of Bishops the bishops of Ghana are reported to have made the following remarks:

> The problem militating against Christian family life in Ghana is Christian marriage itself.
>
> In many African tribal customs, they said, marriage is viewed as a series of steps taken over a long period of time, finally revealed as a lasting bond when the couple has a child. It deeply involves the entire families of the husband and wife and their whole tribal village.
>
> The African bishops' complaint was that Church law and the marriage rite do not in their present form admit adaptation to the African cultural reality in a meaningful way.[18]

These remarks raise the question: What precisely is meant by 'Christian marriage'? It is easy enough to say what the term means in western, European Christianity. But how much of what passes for Christian marriage is Christian and how much of it is western? Is the identification of marriage with a single moment of formal commitment by husband and wife alone a Christian element or merely a notion derived in the main from western patterns of rationalisation and individualisation. If something valuable is gained in those patterns, has anything valuable been lost? Might not Christian marriage in another context be understood more as a process over time and as involving not only the couple but their families and tribes as well? Where in all this is the 'essence' of marriage and where its 'forms'?[19]

Finally, the communion among the Churches still awaits adequate theological and structural expression. The need for these is evident in the *Nota explicative praevia* to the third chapter of *Lumen Gentium*, where an effort is made to say what *communio* means. It is not, we are told, 'some vague feeling (*affectus*), but an *organic reality* which requires a juridical form and at the same time is animated by charity'. From many standpoints this is a very inadequate explanation. Few will maintain that communion is exhausted in vague feelings but surely something more can be said than themselves rather vague references to an 'organic reality', with a juridical form enlivened by charity. Charity, after all, covers a multitude of sins. The history of the images of *caput-corpus* reveals how imprecise the notion of an organic reality is. And to mention a juridical form without reference to other substantive constituents of communion, such as the Word of God, the sacraments, traditons, customs, etc., is to oversimplify greatly.[20]

The need to develop extra-conciliar structures of communion has become clear to many by observing that many post-conciliar documents issued from Rome have received the same sorts of criticism that were levelled at the first drafts presented to the Fathers of Vatican II. This similarity leads one to ask whether Vatican II's transformation of the original drafts is still considered to have been a good thing; if it is, must there not be some regular procedures by which the voices of the Churches can be heard and taken seriously *before* documents affecting the life of the Church universal are issued?

In the end a true communion of the Churches will be possible only when the local and particular Churches assume full responsibility for their own self-realisations. This will mean, first, the development of the synodal principle on the local and particular levels, a process only just beginning, still marked by many imperfections, and still suspect in many quarters.[21] Secondly, it will mean a greater consciousness on the part of the Churches that they are themselves the primary subject of the Church's realisation in their times, places and cultures. On the one hand, it is not clear that the Churches and their bishops always recognise this clearly. At times, in watching television reports of the many papal trips, one wonders if the view is not rather widely shared that today 'thanks to the TV, there is now only one bishop, John-Paul II'.[22] On the other hand, the local Churches have to be given the freedom to act for themselves. Even if one were to grant that the situation in Holland was grave enough to warrant the intervention of Rome, one may still have serious reservations about the instrument devised to address it and one may hope that before it is taken as a precedent for future interventions, it will be made 'the object of careful ecclesiological criticism.

In all these tensions the issue is the question with which we began, whether and how it is true, to adapt a statement of the Council, that 'the variety of the local Churches, united in a common effort (*in unum conspirans varietas*) splendidly displays the catholicity of an undivided Church' (LG § 23).

Notes

1. This is the notion Aquinas used to defend the unity of the sacrament of orders; see *Commentary on the Sentences*, IV, d. 24, 1. 2, a. 1 ad 2m.

2. See Y. Congar 'De la communion des Églises à une ecclésiologie de l'Église universelle' *Lépiscopat et l'Église universelle* (Unam Sanctam, 39; Paris 1971) pp. 227-260.

3. See A. Acerbi *Due ecclesiologie: Ecclesiologia giuridica ed ecclesiologia di communione nella 'Lumen Gentium'* (Bologna 1975).

4. See Bernard Lonergan *Method in Theology* (New York 1972) pp. 79, 356-358.

5. 'We can and must make fast at the outset our understanding of the Church as a body or community of human beings, albeit existing in response to the activity of God. In this sense, the ontology of the Church means in the first instance the humanly subjective pole of the relationship' (Claude Welch *The Reality of the Church* [New York 1958] p. 48).

6. H. Legrand 'Inverser Babel, mission de l'Église' *Spiritus* 43 (1970) 334.

7. Legrand *ibid.* 329.

8. H. deLubac *The Splendour of the Church* (New York 1956) pp. 30-34 (*Méditation sur l'Église,* 2nd ed. Paris 1952).

9. Lonergan *Method in Theology* p. 363.

10. E. Lanne 'L'Église locale et l'Église universelle' *Irenikon* 43 (1970) 481-511.

11. G. Dejaifve *Un tournant décisif de l'ecclésiologie à Vatican II* (Paris 1978) pp. 109-127.

12. *Communicationes* 12 (1980) 80.

13. *Ibid.* 8 (1976) 98-101.

14. *Ibid.* 9 (1977) 288, 290.

15. *Ibid.* 8 (1976) 89.

16. *Ibid.* 8 (1976) 98.

17. *Ibid.* 8 (1976) 102-105; 9 (1977) 84-90, 107-109.

18. *The Catholic News* 93 (16 October 1980) 9.

19. For other examples, see J. N'Dayen 'The Relations of the Local Churches with Rome and the Function of the Episcopal Conference of Black Africa' *The Churches of Africa: Future Prospects*, ed. C. Geffré and B. Luneau (*Concilium* 106 1977) 60-68.

20. For an example of reducing *communio* to *subordinatio* and *consensio*, see *Communicationes* 8 (1976) 103-104, where it is argued that the pope's only choice, should a thousand bishops declare themselves against celibacy, is to declare them excommunicate!

21. In the United States, there have been three examples, the preparation of the National Catechetical Directory and of the Bishops' Statement on Moral Values and the 1976 Call to Action Conference in Detroit. Each of these was seriously flawed, especially in its final stages. For the suspicions aroused in Rome, see *Communicationes* 9 (1977) 285-286.

22. This is the remark, apparently of a French bishop, on the eve of Pope John-Paul's visit to France; see *Informations Catholiques Internationales* 548 (March 1980) 20.

Georg Kretschmar

The Eschatological Tension in the Life of the Church Today

1

THE LIFE of the Church cannot exist without tension between the promise of God for his people and our everyday experience. That is a sentence which combines a dogmatic and an empirical statement. We cannot avoid coming up against this combination when we try to understand the Church in history. The Church appears to the historian and the contemporary as a social union. However, the unity of this social union is not determined by an inherited culture, language community or social structure, even though these are very important for the physical being of the Church, but by a firm belief established by historical tradition. Christians themselves had to speak in terms of a faith which was continually brought to life from the gospel in all places from one generation to another. If it were not so there would be no continuity between a 'Christian civilistion' from which we are, perhaps, descended and a possible forthcoming diaspora existence. Even the impartial historian, when he is dealing with the phenomenon of the Church or of individual churches will not be able to avoid speaking of the conviction, the faith of the Christians though statistical and demoscopic findings may expose the discrepancy between the official and compulsory teaching and that which can be confirmed as relevant for a majority of individual Christians. The discrepancy which is expressed in this statement is not the same as the eschatological tension. But nevertheless it indirectly establishes that for the actual existence of the Church factors other than the identity of a tribe, a nation or a trade union decide the issue. The Church is always dependent on the gospel which has been given to her.

This message, however, points beyond the Church. The word 'gospel' is only a code, an apostolic abbreviation for the promise that in Jesus Christ who was crucified and rose from the dead the promises of God for his creation are fulfilled. The gospel itself is an eschatological message, a promise of salvation for the world and human fulfilment under God in Christ. The mythological, apocalyptic thought of early Christian times may appear to us somewhat more naïve in retrospect than it would have a right to do under closer inspection. These traditions and traditional ways of thinking still concern us, but, as is well known, the old Church had already translated them into the categories of Greek thought and in continuing its mission has continually repeated this process of translation, even though those earlier formulations retain their fundamental significance. However, just as the word 'fulfilment' transcends all possible earthly experience, so all translations of the apocalyptic pictures of antiquity can only have an allusive character. But even such unrenounceable words as 'promise' and 'future' already sum up the time-tension involved. Whoever says that the Church lives from the gospel is virtually saying that this social union is directed to a future which is announced in the present but is not yet obtained by it. This future begins in the Church and therefore the Church can be valued as a new saving reality in a lost world. It is the very eschatological tension that makes it only just a beginning. This has always been a part of the Church but through the changing times it is not always experienced in the same intensity or in the same way. The question is to what extent and where it determines faith, action and hope in our churches today.

We should note that right from the start this hope has had two aspects: the Church looks for her own consummation and for the new creation. If we may understand 'God's kingdom' as a code-word to denote the renewal and bringing home of the world then they are united with one another in the ancient Eucharistic prayers of the *Didache* which date from the end of the first century: 'Remember, Lord, thy Church, deliver her from all evil and make her perfect in thy love. And gather her, this Church thou hast sanctified, from the four winds into thy kingdom which thou hast prepared for her.' (10, 5.) The accent here is on the future of the Church. The well-known definition of the Second Vatican Council also classifies the 'Church', and 'God's kingdom' together although it works with completely different concepts and has the future of the world in view when it describes the Church in Christ as 'being like a sacrament, that is to say a symbol and an instrument for the innermost union with God and for the unity of the whole of humankind' (LG § 1). Both texts may appear as abstract theology. Do we not come nearer to the real life of the Church when we bring both these aspects together and speak in terms of the inadequacy, even of the guilt of the Church and demand that they must take responsibility for the world and be 'churches for the others'? That may be. At first sight at least these more concrete expressions leave the eschatalogical dimension in the shade. Perhaps this is one of the reasons why years of discussion here have achieved so little. But this first impression is deceptive.

2

The Church is still waiting for her own consummation. With regard to individual Christians that is so indisputable that one could speak of a banality if it were not in fact a matter of description and meaning of a whole human life in success, failure and preservation. This is also true of the Christian community, of the Church, which is the mother of the faithful and, therefore, *'ecclesia viatorum'*, the Church on the way, not only in the sense expressed in the famous English hymn: '. . . she waits for consummation. . . . Till with the vision glorious/her longing eyes are blest,/and the great Church victorious/will be the Church at rest'.[1] The promise of victory and of consummation is no guarantee that the Church will be preserved in its entirety. The Augustinian model which proceeded from God's election and described the Church in history as *'corpus permixtum'*, a mixture of good and evil, certainly retains its validity for the obvious reason that the Church is always a community of human beings. However, it is not enough to describe the consummation of the Church primarily as the revelation of her hidden sanctity in the separation of true believers and hypocrites. Even the old controversial theme about the sense in which the (baptised) sinner belongs to the Church loses its meaning here. For us today expectations of consummation comprises a hope in the renewal of the Church. It seems to me that the theological and pastoral task of the present is to bring the manifold expectations of the Church and especially the widespread disappointment in her into this great eschatological hope.

Here we have an unavoidable theological problem. We must learn to speak not only of sinners in the Church or of a Church of sinners, but also of the sins of the Church, not only of her imperfection. This does not mean the slovenly impartiality with which boldly fanciful groups or cabals today occasionally delete former values with the stroke of a pen. No, it is a matter of admitting that actual failure is a fault of the Church and this can be admitted in the certainty that God's forgiveness and our willingness to learn belong to the basic form of grace through which God gathers his Church into his kingdom.[2] Certainly for years people, Christians among them, have spoken of ecclesiastical guilt in connection with such themes as anti-Semitism or compromising pacts made with the leaders of that time. But why have such declarations from individual groups had so little liberating effect when taken as a whole? Traditionally we have few examples of a Church speaking appropriately and credibly of her guilt. Even the ecclesiastical acknowledgement of guilt to which I shall now refer was always a controversial matter. It concerns the declaration made on 18-19 October 1945 in Stuttgart by the Council of the Protestant Church in Germany, founded only seven weeks before that date, to a representative delegation of the Ecumenical Council of the Church, which was also still in its infancy. This spoke of a 'solidarity of guilt' with the German people and was detailed as follows: 'With deep sorrow we say: Through us endless suffering has been inflicted on many peoples and countries. Now, in the name of the whole Church, we state what we have often declared to our congregations. We have indeed fought for many years in the name of Jesus Christ against the spirit which found its fearful expression in the National Socialist régime of power, but we charge ourselves for not having more courageously acknowledged the situation, offered more genuine prayers, believed more piously or loved more ardently.'[3] Historically it is indisputable that this declaration has made a new communion possible with other churches of the Christian faith to the extent that it has 'gathered' the churches together. It did not destroy continuity but established an identity by the acknowledgement of guilt. It should also have been a true act of confession as it explicitly stated that it was 'a matter to be settled between God and us'. It characterised the way in which the failure of the Church was spoken about in terms of the conflict between mission and promise on the one hand and actual conduct on the other. There was reason to regard this as awareness of the eschatological tension. Nevertheless, at that time much remained obscure and in dispute and even the writers and co-signatories gave different explanations. How are ecclesiastical and political guilt related to another? Where is the identity of the speakers here to be found with the entire nation to which they attribute a 'solidarity of guilt'? Is it only in that they were members of the same race? Had they any authority at all to say such things on behalf of others? Or was it a priestly confession for the nation? The signatories themselves were certainly not members of the National Socialist Party. But then would not ecclesiastical identity have been purchased by an imputed solidarity with the nation? In any case, what is meant here by churches? Are we not here speaking of the circle of office-holders who remained true during the evil time rather than of God's people? Have we come back once more to the Augustinian model of the Church as 'corpus permixtum'?

These are not rhetorical questions; they were broached at that time, but were not followed through. The justice and significance of the Stuttgart acknowledgement of guilt should not be lessened by this statement. Nor is it an argument against the declaration that led it to new questions. The fact that these questions remained unanswered contributed to the situation in which the general public, the majority of the baptised, ignored this 'Stuttgart acknowledgement of guilt' and many felt it to be painful rather than liberating. But this is still only one instance of the theme of the identity of a Church that acknowledges her failure as a sin. Certainly there is the phenomenon of an impenitent hierarchy and of congregations which find no help for their understanding from 'those above'. But at that time things were more complicated—although many congregations felt betrayed by this declaration of guilt given by their bishops. However, the real problem is that it is so difficult to mediate insights in the sphere in which we most strongly experience eschatological tension as a failure of the Church in relation to her mission. Where does the Church stand in relation to such lack of communication? Even in this kind of confusion, however, it still holds good that the Church can only renew herself when she is ready to live from forgiveness at all levels and in all her organisations and to declare this. This is not a formula to resolve difficulties but an agenda of action. When the Church seeks her own consummation she can only look away from herself to the God who has assembled her through faith and baptism, that is through Christ in the Holy Ghost, and who alone can make her pefect even through her failure and guilt.

3

What, on the other hand, did seem to be a releasing formula for many was the statement Dietrich Bonhoeffer made from his imprisonment in Tegel, which said that the Church had to learn to be a 'Church for others'. In his 'Outline of Work' of the summer of 1944 he drew up the following sketch: 'Our relationship with God is not one of a "religious" attitude to the highest, most powerful and supreme being imaginable—that is not a genuine transcendence—our relationship with God is a new life of "existence for others", of participation in the being of Christ.' From this it follows that: 'The Church is only a Church if it is there for others. In order to make a start she must send all her possessions to the poor and needy. Her ministers must live exclusively from the voluntary gifts of the community and if necessary practise a worldly profession. She must take part in the worldly tasks of the human life of the community, not officioulsy but helpfully and humbly. She must tell people of all professions what it is "to be for others".'[4] That is a model which the Church immediately appeared to decry only to turn round and ask herself about her own identity and perfection. The eschatological theme is service to the world. The eschatological tension proceeds from the fact that the Church has to understand, through suffering and learning, that God is also at work in the world around her. Only in stepping beyond herself can she be an authentic tool for bringing the world home, not in the Church, but in God, her Creator. Bonhoeffer's train of thought is closer to the formula of the Second Vatican Council of the Church as a 'symbol and instrument for the innermost union with God and for the whole of humankind' than we would expect. Indeed, for the man in the cell Christ is pushed so far into isolation that he does not write of the Church as a symbol, but as a human model. The question of the identity of the Church, in fact of her sacramentality, is not hereby rejected, it just comes up in another dimension. Bonhoeffer spoke of this in intimations, above all under the sign of the *disciplina arcani*, the discipline of the secret.[5] To this day Bonhoeffer's outline has lost none of its relevance. The cry for a poor Church and Church for the poor has swelled beyond expectations, but with a new accent. 'Churches for the others' has become a cry which individuals and groups have transformed into political and social activities in solidarity with the poor of the world. This has not always been connected with the eschatological tension in the life of the Church today. But it will be experienced when one asks about the specific task of the Church with regard to service to the world. This service, with which the Church either stands or falls, has been the preaching of the gospel of Christ since the days of the apostles and is combined with intercession and acts of love—not the changing of the world into a new society. But the preaching of the gospel at any given time happens under definite social conditions and changes them at the same time. The responsibility of love for one's neighbour is not exhausted in individual acts of charity. Even the intercession, in order to be real, needs to examine the situation. The tension then grows from the fact that the specific mission of the Church to serve others transcends not only the Church but also the native tendencies of society and will be fulfilled in that very society with all the means of fulfilment which it has at its disposal. The obligation to co-operate with 'others' and to maintain the Church's own independence results from this—not out of a concern about its image, but from mission.

As a rule this is experienced in particular experiences. It is well known that the churches in South Africa are divided in their attitudes towards the Apartheid ideology of the Boers; and also that many churches, especially in Namibia, incline towards the African freedom movement. This is certainly not only a case of arbitrary political judgment, it is a matter of conscience. Judged by the criterion of the gospel, it is certainly no small matter that the boundaries of churches and therefore of concrete communions are determined by the colour of people's skin. Under such conditions, which do allow no one any permanent neutrality with regard to the conflict, one way in which ecclesiastical responsibility is shown is that the situation also comes up for consideration after a possible change of power and that those now in power may become the oppressed with the result that precautions need to be taken now against the danger of a reversal of racial discrimination. Such considerations on the part of African churchmen are already causing a rift between them and both the rulers of today and the military liberation movements.

In a completely different way the same tension shows itself in the questions which are always being asked: To what extent should a Church build and maintain its own institutions for social commitments, from kindergartens to schools and hospitals, and to what extent should the Christian work in pluralistic establishments of that kind run by the State or by some other organisation? In West Germany it is being discussed whether Church workers should organise themselves in the form of general trade unions or whether they should develop their own form in order to settle social conflicts as there is no place in the Church for strikes. The decisions in the particular case will always fall within the limits of the conditioning factors of the time. But when one must proceed from the fact that God's people in the world have to be a serving community one will not be able to disguise the fact that there are disputes in our society as to what help for people really is, for example help for a woman who has an unwanted pregnancy. As a rule such disputes will be an argument for the construction of independent Christian social establishments. But we cannot exclude the tensions and conflicts of the society. Attempts to reach a solution can then acquire a model character, become themselves a form of service to 'others'. But the Church does not have the promise that her schools or hospitals shall be better than those under other management any more than the individual Christian has been promised that he will be a more capable worker, tradesman or doctor than his non-Christian colleagues. And yet the world remains a society, a field of trial assigned to the Church and the Christian. The eschatological tension in the life of the churches is reflected in these contradictory statements.

These last considerations should make it clear that both aspects belong to hope, that the Church is still waiting for her consummation and at the same time it is called upon to serve in the world. Only a Church that lives from forgiveness can be a Church for others and will in this way preserve her identity, for this identity is founded only in the mission through Christ and the gift of the Spirit.

Translated by Jean Allan

Notes

1. From 'The Church's one foundation' by S. S. Wesley, 1864.

2. That is not an opinion on the question of the fallibility or infallibility of the Church, but a statement on how God keeps his Church in the truth.

3. Quoted from: Armin Boyens *Kirchenkampf und Ökumene 1939-1945. Darstellung und Dokumentation* (Munich 1973) p. 361.

4. *Widerstand und Ergebung* ed. E. Bethge, new edition (Munich 1970) p. 414 ff.

5. Letter of 30 April 1944 to E. Bethge (p. 306); of 5 May 1944 also to E. Bethge: 'There are degrees of knowledge and significance; that is, we must re-establish a *disciplina arcani* through which the secrets of the Christian faith will be protected from profanity' (p. 312); compare: 'Gedanken zum Tauftag', May 1944 (especially p. 328).

D

PART II

Messianic Signs in History

D. S. Amalorpavadass

The Poor with No Voice and No Power

'THE POOR' constitute a major concern not only in the Judaeo-Christian tradition but also in the religious traditions of the countries of Asia and in our contemporary history and society. It is a theme running through the entire Bible.

1. 'THE POOR', AN ATTRACTIVE THEME

The poor are a group with whom Communists and other ideological groups try to identify themselves and whose cause they claim to espouse. Politicians of all colour and shape try to advance their own political ambitions by shouting slogans and making promises connected with the poor. But the poor have been shrewd enough to see through these gimmicks. They are now in a process of disillusionment and refuse to be subject to such brain-washing.

In the Church itself, 'the poor', 'the Church of the poor', 'witness of poverty' and 'simple and poor life-style' became central themes at the peak moments of the Second Vatican Council.

Ever since questions like 'what is religious poverty?', 'who are the poor?', 'what is the Church of the poor?' have absorbed the attention of various groups in the Church. The review *Concilium* itself has devoted several of its issues to this theme.

It is against this background that we are invited to reflect on the poor, the group of people who have no voice and no power.

2. POVERTY: A POSITIVE CONCEPT AND A TOTAL REALITY

In a comprehensive view and understanding, poverty is a positive concept and a total reality: first of all, it is a triangle of Reality; secondly, it is constitutive of humanisation of people. Christian discipleship and religious life; and thirdly, it has a triple implication.

(*a*) **First of all, poverty is a triangle of Reality:** It should be situated and understood:

(i) against the background of religious traditions and cultural heritage of India and

45

other Asian countries; it is the flowing stream of our people's age-old quest for Moksha (Release);

(ii) with reference to the reality of social injustice in contemporary India and Third World countries: the reality of Indian society today in its state of dependence and social injustice constitutes problem number one for the country and for the world. The poor do not have a place in the present society and hence their struggle for a new and just society;

(iii) and in the light of biblical revelation: it calls for a spiritual discernment and theological interpretation of 'poverty' and the 'poor'.

They are three angles of a single reality, and their convergence makes a single whole (triangle) and define poverty adequately.

The theme under all its three aspects is definitely comprehensive, positive and converging. They are interpenetrative of one another and dynamically make a single and coherent whole. They are sharply challenging and relevantly practical.

(b) **Secondly, poverty is constitutive of:** (a) humanisation of people; (b) Christian discipleship; and (c) religious life.

Poverty is at the core of Christian discipleship and it is also its cost. As such it is an indispensable element of Christian life and a requisite of Church renewal according to the vision and programme of Vatican II. It implies a correct scale of values and a definite order of priority. It calls for a radical understanding of the gospel and the kingdom, for a clear option and a readiness to take risks. It consists in losing oneself for the sake of the gospel and the kingdom, in the total and unreserved following of Jesus, the Master.

Poverty is also the constitutive element or essence of religious life. As both an exigency and consequence of religious life, poverty is an all-round freedom and total availability for the service of all. In this service, the religious are truly 'the poor' and thereby yearn for another world and for a new society, and hence work to enter into the new order of things, the kingdom which is opening before them right now.

Both Christian discipleship and religious life will be hollow and baseless unless they embody authentic and full-fledged humanity. A Christian and a religious are primarily genuine human persons and hence should have undergone a process of humanisation. They should continue the same as they try to live their Christian discipleship and religious commitment.

(c) **Thirdly, the theme of poverty has a triple implication,** exigency and consequence in dynamic tension and dialectical interaction as a result of a spiritual discernment and theological interpretation.

Moksha (Release) as self-realisation and God-realisation becomes the goal.

Dharma (Justice) liberation and social justice, humanisation of men and creation of a 'dharmic' (just) society are the immediate objectives.

Ashram: It is expressed in a life-style of poverty and simplicity, in genuine identification with the poor.

The above can be expressed better in the diagram at the top of page 47.

3. POVERTY AS A TRIANGLE OF REALITY

(a) The 'Poor' Against the Background of Indian Religious Traditions

It is a vast subject. For our purpose it will suffice to take for consideration a few major trends and key-concepts in the religious quest of India.

First of all, life flows like a river. We need to plunge ourselves into it and be carried

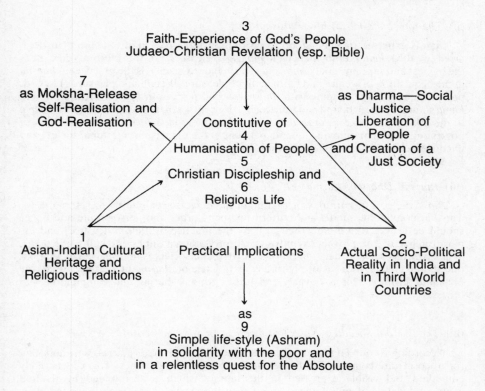

3
Faith-Experience of God's People
Judaeo-Christian Revelation (esp. Bible)

7
as Moksha-Release
Self-Realisation and
God-Realisation

Constitutive of
4
Humanisation of People
5
Christian Discipleship and
6
Religious Life

as Dharma—Social
Justice
Liberation of
People
and Creation of a
Just Society

1
Asian-Indian Cultural
Heritage and
Religious Traditions

Practical Implications

2
Actual Socio-Political
Reality in India and
in Third World
Countries

as
9
Simple life-style (Ashram)
in solidarity with the poor and
in a relentless quest for the Absolute

forward. Such is the *religious tradition and cultural heritage of India*, or of any other country for that matter.

(i) *Moksha*

Life and history are considered in India as a journey (*yatra*) and its ultimate goal is to obtain *moksha*—release from the endless cycle of life (birth and re-birth) and to enjoy full liberation. The goal to be reached is the most important reality. Therefore it can be compared to a target to be hit in one go with the arrow from the bow. In order to reach the end, one should choose the path (*marga*) and walk on it, and one should adapt the means (*sadhana*) and practise it regularly. In the understanding of *Gnana marga*, the path of contemplative wisdom, ignorance or lack of awareness (*avidya*) is the root cause of all evil and enslavement. The removal of it is the way to *moksha*, and the means to remove it is knowledge. It is an intuitive and mystical knowledge (*vidya*). This is liberation and this is the realisation of self (*Atman-Jeevatman*) as well as the realisation of the Absolute (*Brahman* or *Paramatman*) in the ultimate unity of all.

This is the radicality of Indian spirituality and religious life. Here is the connection between poverty and *moksha*. The 'poor' are those who, for the sake of pursuing and reaching the goal detach themselves from all other realities. These *gnanayogis* are indeed poor and become voiceless and powerless for they are in all-round wholeness (silence) and in fullness of power (possessing God and achieving liberation).

(ii) *The fourfold goals of life (Purusharthas)*

Man is expected or understood to pursue fourfold goals in life: *dharma* (justice), *artha* (wealth), *kama* (enjoyment) and *moksha* (release, liberation). From Vedic times the highest and supreme goal is *moksha*. The means to reach it is the practice of *dharma* in the acquisition of wealth and enjoyment of pleasure. Wealth and pleasure are good, provided they are in keeping with *dharma*, social justice. In other words, *artha* and *kama* should be so regulated and transcended by *dharma* that they all become conducive to the attainment of *moksha* (*artha-dharma-kama* and *moksha*). One cannot think of possessing wealth or enjoying life independent of the universe, forgetful of society and unconcerned about one's brothers and sisters.

(iii) *Rta and Dharma, Karma*

Rta is the cosmic harmony or rhythm in the universe realised by the eternal Law. This harmony is the model and pattern for social order and personal life and hence should be reflected and embodied in it by the practice of *dharma* (justice) and the performance of *karma* (one's family, social, professional duties and cultic practices). Whenever this social order (*dharma*) is violated and society is in disharmony with *rta*, one should change it or restore harmony by practice of *dharma* in a disinterested way (*niskama karma*). This is poverty and justice, this is sharing and communion with others.

(iv) *The fivefold Sheathes (Kosas) of macrocosm and microcosm*

According to our Hindu understanding both the universe (macrocosm) and man (microcosm) are composed of five elements or layers or sheathes. This is concretely embodied and visibly expressed in the temple which is surrounded by fivefold compound walls and ambulatories (*avaranas*). In the agamic spirituality, the temple is the symbolic representation of the structure of this world and the individual in the heart of both of which dwells the supreme spirit (*Brahman*).

Now a visit to the temple in pilgrimage or for performance of worship (*puja*) is a process of movement in concentric circles and interiorisation of the self till one reaches the sanctuary of the temple, *mulasthanam* (converging centre) or *garba-graha* (womb), where the deity (the Lord) dwells and where his *dharshan* can be had. Thus detachment from the five *kosas* is in view of attachment to the Lord. Transcendence of *kosas* is for the sake of immanence with God. Poverty is therefore acquisition of universality and communion. The poor are those who are one with others and with God by a process of detachment in the movement towards higher goals.

(v) *The four ashramas of life*

If life is a pilgrimage, it consists of stages. One has fullness of life and reaches one's ultimate goal by passing through four stages: *Brahmacharya*, the state of discipleship and initiation to adult life through the study of Vedas and seeking Brahman. *Grahasthya* the state in which one gets married and becomes a householder to involve one's self in the world and fulfil one's duties in family, society and profession according to various forms of *dharma*. While so doing one could get engrossed in life and forget the ultimate goal. Hence one retires into the forest with one's family for a spiritual renewal, *Vanaprasthya*. Even this is not ideal as one is divided in one's attention. Hence one enters into the fourth and final state, a life of total renunciation (*Sannyasa*).

Even if one does not physically pass through these four stages, at least the values and emphases of these stages should be embodied and lived in each one's life.

(vi) *Sannyasa*

The last of the four stages of life consists in complete renunciation of the world and total surrender to the ultimate. It is a total abandonment of everything in view of possessing God by self-realisation and God-experience. The *Sannyasis* are embodiments of the supreme and the ultimate. God-realisation is the main content of *Sannyasa*. Hence they are not supposed to know or teach anything other than God-experience. As a *jeevan-mukta*, as one who has reached the other shore of life, he does not belong to this world and has no place in this society. Thereby he marginalises himself away from the centre of power, influence and prestige, maintains silence and communicates through silence. In this sense the *Sannyasis* are also the poor of India and therefore are voluntarily 'powerless and voiceless'.

(vii) *Ashram*

All that we have said above is in some sense summed up and institutionalised in what is called 'Ashram'. It is the embodiment of all the ideals in terms of life-style. It is a state or place of intense and sustained spiritual quest for the Absolute by a group of persons around and under the guidance of a guru. This is fostered by renunciation and detachment, in an atmosphere of silence, peace and joy. The life-style here is necessarily simple, in conformity with Indian tradition and context and as a genuine expression of a life of contemplation. It is dedicated to prayer and/or service. It is open to all and welcomes men and women of all religions, status and race. The ashramites are therefore authentically poor and qualify for the description as powerless and voiceless. Yet they have a spiritual and moral power, and their life-style is more eloquent than their voice!

From the above reflection one can draw the following conclusions: Material poverty is indispensable for and is an expression of spirit of poverty. It implies sharing with others and voluntarily giving away to those who need. It is synonymous with God-experience or self-realisation (*sat-cit-ananda*). So poverty is meaningless without cosmic dimension, communitarian concern and spiritual experience.

Hence the radical exigency of poverty and the challenges it poses to religious persons to be truly and really 'poor' and opt to be 'powerless and voiceless'.

(b) The 'Poor' with Reference to the Reality of the Third World

To understand the poor, it is not enough to refer to Asian or Indian religious tradition and culture. It is necessary to refer to the social reality of India, of Asia and other Third World countries.

Whether it is at the macro-level of the world, Asia and India, or at the micro-level of village and city, we find ourselves in a society which is marked by poverty and ignorance, oppression and exploitation, enslavement and injustice of all sorts. Nearly 20 per cent of the world's population are rich and dominant, owning and enjoying 80 per cent of the wealth in land and capital and benefiting by most of the goods of the world and fruits of development. They hold all power and wield all influence in all spheres of life; socio-economic, political, cultural and educational. Thus they cause poverty and misery to others. The 80 per cent are poor and dominated, victims of the social mechanism and subject to various forms of injustice. In India alone, nearly 70 per cent are illiterate and 50 per cent live below the poverty line or subsistence level. This half of Indian society or of the Third World is dehumanised, reduced to non-existence and non-persons. They have been marginalised in their own society, having no place or rôle or existence in it. Consciously or unconsciously, overtly or covertly, religion, culture and education seem to have played an ideological rôle giving meaning to the present system, legitimising the status quo, at times facilitating social control and promising compensation in the next world.

This all-round dependence of the masses on the dominant minority and the various forms of injustice done to others is the real source of the oppression and suffering of the masses. It is not only a question of unjust persons and groups but also of unjust structures whether economic, social or political. One has to deal with a systemic evil, structural injustice, organised oppression and institutionalised violence.

The Church as a community of Christians and as an institution is not neutral, nor any other religion for that matter. As constitutive of the human society and working within its structures the Church is plainly and simply a part of the unjust society. There is no such thing as neutrality in an inter-connected and inter-acting complex mechanism that society is. For not to decide is to decide; not to speak out, is to approve of; not to be with the exploited is to be with the exploiters; not to be solidary with the dominated is to support the dominant.

In this situation, the vast majority of our people by being reduced to non-persons and marginalised from the mainstream of society is made to be powerless and voiceless! They become helpless and their situation is hopeless. There is no use in their speaking. If they dared speak it would be either not heard or ignored as nobody would care for what they say. Or they will be silenced by the threat and violence of the dominant group. Thus the oppressed masses could get resigned to their lot, attribute it to their fate, and develop and grow into a culture of silence and impotence. It would appear in their agony that not only men but even God ignores their cry. The silence of men and their lack of reaction might seem to be coupled with the very silence of God as sometimes manifested in the attitudes and reactions of 'religious' people, religious institutions, leaders and communities.

(c) Biblical Understanding of the Poor as 'Powerless' or 'Voiceless'

On the one hand according to Indian religious tradition, some people become poor by a voluntary detachment from earthly goods and a total renunciation of everything, due to their single-minded and relentless religious quest for *moksha* (release) and finding everything in God. This voluntary poverty and simple life-style become a condition and a consequence of God-experience and self-realisation. By their becoming poor, voluntarily they become powerless and voiceless. On the other hand, according to the social analysis of the reality in Asia, a small dominant group of the rich and the powerful reduces the vast majority to the condition of 'poor' and 'destitutes'. In that condition and as a consequence they are made powerless and voiceless.

Against this double background, we need to discern who the real 'poor' are according to the Bible, how they constitute a messianic sign in history, in what sense they are powerless and voiceless, and how the revolution of God's kingdom makes them powerful and eloquent. If so, what is this power, what is the message of their eloquence and what is the good news powerfully proclaimed and eloquently voiced by them?

In the Old Testament we find two connotations for the 'poor'. The first meaning is those who are *materially poor*, the destitute. The Hebrew word *anaw* and the Greek word *ptōchos* refer to the poor as oppressed and exploited, humiliated and enslaved, to victims of injustice, to those dehumanised and made non-persons and those reduced to the condition of diminished worth and capacity not by their mistake but by the action of the dominant. The second meaning evolves from the first. The concept of the poor as destitutes, materially poor and oppressed undergoes a change and gets a *religious or spiritual connotation* during and after the exile. The poor are those who are humble and simple, who do not rely on themselves but place their entire trust in God, and look up to him for their protection and deliverance. This is spirit of poverty and poverty of spirit or religious poverty. It is a detachment from earthly goods and human power and an attachment to God and a reliance on him and his saving action.

Now these two meanings are not exclusive; they converge to give a correct and comprehensive notion of the 'poor'. Spiritual poverty is based on material poverty. One cannot assert that with the experience of destitution and oppression, one will necessarily and always trust in God. Yet it is this experience of being nobody and having no worth and it is the state of powerlessness and voicelessness that makes them turn to the power of God and to cry to him for help and intervention, and to hope for transformation and liberation. On the part of God, he does not ingore or forget them; instead he comes to them, takes charge of them. He sides with the poor, espouses their cause and is determined to change their condition and bring about a new and fraternal society.

In the New Testament Jesus is not neutral either. He embodies God's preference for the poor. He identifies himself with them and takes a clear stand on their behalf. Poverty and destitution are the cost of Christian discipleship. To be a disciple of Christ and to be poor are synonymous (Matt. 10; Luke 9:1-6). The disciples of Jesus have to be poor and should suffer for the sake of becoming and in being the disciples of Christ. To be a disciple means to be identified with the master (the disciple is not above the master; it is enough for him to be like the master), to have the values of the gospel and to be worthy of the kingdom, God's gratuitous and free gift of love. Such a life implies option for values and with priority. And this will lead to conflict, challenge and risk, chiefly at the practical level. The risk involved is calumny and persecution. They will become victims of oppression and injustice; they will be isolated and exiled, ostracised and marginalised in society; and finally they could be killed. This following of Jesus, among other things, also includes detachment from riches. The story of the rich young man (Mark 10:17-22) is striking in this regard. Though he wanted to follow Jesus he could not give up his property and share it with the poor. Riches are an insurmountable obstacle to salvation. Riches make a man self-centred, forgetful of God, a practical atheist and a heartless person, closed to his neighbours and insensitive to the poor. He not only dehumanises others but dehumanises himself first and this paves the way for domination and oppression. This is set in relief in the parable of the rich fool (Luke 12:16-21).

Now the mission and ministry of Jesus are defined with reference to the poor. In his inaugural sermon in the synagogue of Nazareth he releases the manifesto of his ministry (Luke 4:16-21). As they were listening to his talk, God's intervention on behalf of the poor was taking place; a new age was dawning: the final era of salvation history was ushered in; a new society, God's kingdom, his final and universal rule was inaugurated, and a new order of things was erupting in the midst of the old world. Jesus announced his ministry as one of preaching the good news to the poor, heralding freedom to the captives, sight to the blind and liberty to the oppressed. The salvation and liberation announced by Jesus is comprehensive: political-socio-economic, spiritual-religious, historical and eschatological, earthly and heavenly. This social orientation of his mission was confirmed by Jesus in the reply he gave to John's disciples on his identity as the Messiah (Luke 7:18-23; Matt. 11:2-6). The significance of his mission is affirmed beyond doubt and highlighted in his beatitudes as recorded by Luke.

The beatitudes in the Lucan version (6:20-23) in comparison with the Matthaean version (Matt. 5:1-12) is addressed *primarily and directly* to the poor as real destitutes, materially dispossessed and utterly needy, the poor understood as victims of injustice, as marginalised and as living in inhuman conditions of life below subsistence level. It also includes *secondarily* and *consequently* those who are spiritually poor, those who rely on God and look up to him for change of their condition, and who cry to him for intervention and liberation. The three beatitudes of Luke make in fact a single beatitude. 'Happy the Poor', namely the poor and the oppressed are blessed. 'Happy' hereafter and happy even from now on, because the kingdom of God which he proclaims and which he inaugurates with his coming is truly and exclusively theirs (Luke 6:20-21).

The poor are declared happy not because their poverty, the consequence of oppression and injustice, is a good thing, but because his ministry and the arrival of God's kingdom put an end to this evil. The poor are 'happy' because they are to be poor no more. For a total revolution has been launched in their favour and for their benefit and it is sweeping the whole world. The kingdom that is dawning is theirs, they alone can enter into it. The kingdom is the state in which men open themselves totally to God, and accept his fatherly, unconditional and gratuitous love. Under its impact they will radiate and relay that love to all men as brothers and sisters, build up a community of freedom and thus bring about a new fellowship through sharing. This revolution will liberate all men, both the poor and the rich, the oppressed and the oppressors, for all need to be saved and hence all should look to God for security, justice and liberation. It will liberate them from all forms of oppression.

Conclusion

In this kingdom, in the new community of freedom, in this universal fellowship, in this brotherhood and sisterhood, all persons will be powerful and all will have a voice! The power of the poor is the power of the liberating God and the dynamism of his creative and saving Word. The voice of the poor is the voice of the Spirit, the voice of jubilation and the voice of proclaiming the good news of God's marvels on behalf of the poor. In this sense the Canticle of Mary, the *Magnificat*, is the song of the kingdom, the anthem of the new age, the clarion call of the revolution. It is the praise of the poor, who hitherto powerless and voiceless will now voice the marvel of the powerful one (Luke 1:46-53):

> 'My soul proclaims the greatness of the Lord because he has looked upon his lowly handmaid. The Almighty has done great things for me. He has shown the power of his arm, He has pulled down the princes from their thrones and exalted the lowly.'

Mushete Ngindu

The Church of Christendom
in the face of New Cultures

1. A SIGN OF THE TIMES

THE PROBLEM of the inculturation of Christianity is highly topical. Especially in the young churches numerous investigations and viewpoints of a more or less acceptable nature have focused on it. It is one of the questions which the African bishops see as fundamental to the evangelisation of the present-day world, but it is difficult to elicit one particular tendency from all the discussion.

After long reflection on evangelisation in connection with the 1974 Synod of Bishops, the bishops of Africa and Madagascar who attended it issued a statement from which I select the following for special consideration: 'Any action undertaken to build up our churches should pay continual attention to the life of our communities. It is on the basis of these communities that we shall contribute to catholicity not only our specific cultural and artistic experiences . . . but an authentic theological thinking which tries to answer the questions posed by our various historical contexts and by the present development of our societies—a theology which is both loyal to the authentic tradition of the Church, aware of the life of our Christian communities and attentive to our traditions and our languages; that is, to our philosophies.'[1]

In this conception of evangelisation the bishops of Africa and Madagascar 'find a certain theology of adaptation quite out-of-date as against a theology of incarnation. The young churches of Africa and Madagascar cannot ignore this basic requirement. Admitting in effect theological pluralism in the unity of faith, they must encourage by every means a properly African form of theological research. An African theology which is open to the fundamental aspirations of the African peoples will lead Christianity to an effective form of incarnation in the life of the peoples of the Black continent.'[2]

These ideas were taken up and developed in 1975 by the SCEAM Holy Year meeting in Rome (The Symposium of the Episcopal Conferences of Africa and Madagascar). I single out the following from the final resolutions of the conference: 'We recommend that the African episcopate should consider and pronounce on the question of indigenisation; that is, the incarnation of Christ's message, as a problem which is essential to the evangelisation of the continent, just as it is essential to the evangelisation of any part of the world. It is only by means of effective indigenisation that the Christian religion is able to fulfil its claim to be a universal religion.'[3]

The texts that I have just quoted express both the emotivity, the complexity and the range of the phenomenon of the inculturation of Christianity.

Above all three works: *Emancipation d'églises sous tutelle. Essaies sur l'ère post-missionnaire*, by the Cameroonian Meinard P. Hebga,[4] *Le Discours théologique négro-africain. Probleme des fondements*, by the Zaïreian O. Biswemi Kweshi,[5] *Jalons pour une théologie africaine. Essai d'une herméneutique du vodou dahoméen*, by the Benin theologian B. AdoKounou,[6] numerous articles in journals, a wide range of themes, ideas and formulations are evidence of creative power and a movement which is constantly growing. Clergy and laity, as well as religious are inspired by a veritable grass-roots movement of great power.

In the following pages I shall try to elicit the significance of this movement by examining successively and schematically:

1. the process of transmission of the gospel message;
2. the ways in which our churches are implicated in the process of colonisation;
3. the prospects for a new missionary era.

2. THE PROCESS OF TRANSMISSION OF THE GOSPEL MESSAGE

In each era the Church is faced with the same problem: how to present the gospel message to minds which have undergone change. How to find the means to respond to new questions posed by the sciences and to new problems of conscience?

This is a delicate and many-faceted problem, but it has never been posed with more urgency than in the last few decades. 'Quite apart from the new positive appreciation of the major non-Christian religions since Vatican II, awareness of the diverse historical forms taken by Christianity has never been so intense. Never has awareness of a certain barrier to its claim to universality been so evident and never has the discovery of religious and cultural realities which are alien to the Christian West been so strong', is the finding of C. Geffré and J.-P. Jossua.[7]

That is not all. All those changes which may be subsumed under the title of scientific and technological progress would seem to have occurred without the influence of the Church, sometimes even in spite of the injunctions or threats of its leaders. The institutional development of the religious sciences, alongside theology and scholastic philosophy, was perhaps the fact of most concern to the Christian and above all Catholic consciousness in the last years of the nineteenth century in Europe. This fact is at the root of the religious crisis which shook the Catholic Church in this period. It was a crisis which entered history under the equivocal term 'modernism'.[8] In our own days that which contradicts the action of the gospel is not at all what might properly be termed a heresy, nor an aggressive negation (although heresy still holds sway over considerable areas, and in certain areas militant atheism may exist in an organised form), but a diffuse form of thought immanent in all those new instruments with which reason has equipped itself (machines, political institutions, critical methodologies, and so on), and which are tantamount to a system. What term one uses to describe this system—whether liberalism, rationalism or idealism—is of little concern; it always amounts to a doctrine centred upon the cult of man made God, and not on the worship of God made man.

The problem of the inculturation of Christianity is, however, posed with special urgency in regard to the young churches of the Third World, which have no Athens and Rome as their cultural roots. It is not only a question of *adaptation*, of renewal within one and the same advancing culture. It is a matter of constructing a comprehensive and explanatory theology, a theology in which local cultures are not merely described but actually integrated into a larger conceptual whole, allowing a critical examination of the fundamentals of Christian revelation (*Ad Gentes,* § 22). This is an extremely difficult task and one for which historical information and goodwill are not a sufficient condition. There is a great and constant risk that religious truth will be confused with the systems of thought which historically it has used to express itself.[9] As Fr Bimwenyi has remarked in regard to Africa, 'Dialogue does not take place between the African past and our present in regard to our future, between the past of Africa and its suffering present, but between the present of Africa and the present of the West, as well as the past of that very same West'. Moreover: 'The Christian part of the West cannot be laid claim to by Africa as its authentic past because Africa was not part of it, and therefore did not share in the ancient heresies and schisms which we are aware of only through evangelisation, and which we nevertheless experience: Protestants, Orthodox and Catholics all come, with a passionate faith in Jesus Christ, but divided among themselves, throwing stones at one another and asking us to do almost the same thing or worse . . . this is the burden which we have inherited. It is an heritage which we find burdensome in more than one respect. For us it is a matter of discerning and eliciting the message of God, which is always the same, addressed to all ages and to all nations: a message which should reach the African consciousness and allow it to *renew itself in a vital way from within*, by exercising the four basic functions of any community which springs from the Word of God . . . the liturgical or cultural function, the ethical or moral function, the juridical function, and the theological function.'[10]

We might say indeed that there are only two possible methods for establishing a connection between tradition and the present, between old and new, between the Word of God and human minds. Two methods—that is, two ways of thinking, two types of action, two solutions to the problem.

The first method consists, *first and above all*, of establishing what is tradition (in short, the history of the identity of Christian truth), in order to possess it soundly and to be able to understand it appropriately both in regard to formulations and to spirit, and even more precisely in the spirit of its formulations; then to turn our gaze to the thought of the world in which we live in order to see it in all its aspects, in the letter and in the spirit, in order to discover whatever in it may accord with—and whatever may contradict—the spirit of tradition, assimilating the first component, which is substantial, and rejecting the second, which is corrupt.

The second method consists in establishing, *first and above all*, present thought, of borrowing its language, of drawing on its principles, and filling ourselves with its spirit; then in looking at tradition, in order finally to reject everything in it which seems contrary to present-day thought, and to adapt to it what remains.

These are the principles of the two methods. I shall now examine the consequences.

In the first case, we either obtain a confirmation of tradition and of the modes of expression of tradition, and therefore a new knowledge of its riches, or a new expression which brings precision to the traditional exposition and which, permitting of an improved ability to discern associated but corrupt doctrines, helps us the better to possess and practise it.

In the second case we obtain an expression of tradition which tradition itself would not recognise. For the form of expression is not only new but its novelty indicates a form of corruption and not increased precision. If it remains identical, its original meaning is lost because a contradictory interpretation disfigures it and empties it of substance.

The first method is practised by those whom we might call orthodox reformers or, better still, Christian thinkers. It is tantamount to giving Christian thought a new form of expression which retains its spirit. It is the method of an Athanasius, an Aquinas and a Newman.

The second method is that of the heterodox reformers whom one might with more justice entitle 'innovators'. . . . It is tantamount to giving a religion a new form contrary to the spirit, and therefore to creating a new religion, different from that which was intended by the founder. This is the method of an Arius or a Loisy, for example.

These two solutions and two methods which I have presented schematically may at first sight offer similarities which mislead the spirit. A thinker may even believe that he or she has adopted the first when he or she is engaged in the second. Above all one may slide imperceptibly from first to second and find oneself involuntarily in the enemy camp. Without anticipating the future too much, we may say that this tragic experience has often been the lot of those who have been called modernists. Because of an inadequate philosophical and religious training, they allowed themselves to pass from orthodoxy to heterodoxy without discerning the exact moment of crossing the Rubicon.

This is a warning to take care when assessing forms of thought which are in the making. When a product of thought is ready, it is possible to see to what kind of reform it belongs, but such discernment is difficult at the beginning and in the initial stages. That is what we read in the gospel (Matt. 13:23-30). The grain and the chaff cannot be separated at first, and in removing the chaff one runs the risk of removing the grain at the same time.

3. THE IMPLICATION OF OUR CHURCHES IN THE HISTORICAL PROCESS OF COLONISATION

We are beginning to see more precisely that in a general way, and in spite of missionary generosity, the evangelisation of the Third World took place in a context of violence and oppression. A few examples will suffice to illustrate this rather extreme proposition.

The conquest of Latin America began when the conquest of Spain was at an end. The great discoveries and the great conquests began with the end of the reconquest of Islam by Christendom. The ambiguity of this historical situation is well known. Evangelisation served to advance or to justify the great adventure of conquest; the popes empowered the kings of Portugal and Spain to evangelise the world which they were in the process of conquering.

Let us hear what Dussel has to say on this subject: 'The Christendom of the Indies, located on the periphery, is colonial. The adjective "colonial" is necessary. We are the only colonial Christendom. Moreover, to discover in what sense we are "colonial" is to discover on the theological, philosophical and historical level exactly what we are as Latin American Christians. To cease to be "colonial" is to free oneself, to universalise oneself, but not under the oppression of a specific culture. It was only after the 1962 Council that it became possible, after passing beyond the limits of the Mediterranean culture, to respond to a form of evangelisation which will bring us, as I hope, universal conversion: that is, the conversion of Africa and Asia.'[11]

African Christianity, as we know, is intimately linked to the colonial situation and suffers from the ambiguity of that situation. Why not emphasise the fact? The evangelisation of Africa occurred in a context of violence and legitimised reduction of the African peoples and their identity. The missionaries did not know (how could they?) how to surrender a *tabula rasa* approach and take seriously the African man with his fundamental aspirations, and his special visions of the world, man and God. It is a cherished thesis of the Société Africaine de Culture that in all the links established between Africa and Europe, that is what occurred and continued to occur in regard to universal humanity.[12]

This may seem a rather harsh judgment. It is historically grounded. The evangelisation of the Third World, to return to Dussel, grossly ignored 'the other'. An entire part of the Christian world was built on a negation of the humanity of the human worlds which it discovered. When one travels through Latin America it is distressing to see what has been done there by the 'civilising mission' of the colonialists and the religious agents who followed them. Entire peoples were integrated into the Church without asking themselves who they were, what they were looking for and what they aspired to.

4. THE PROSPECTS OF THE NEW MISSIONARY AGE

It is not masochism or some guilt complex that forces us to recall this sad history. It is so that the truth should emerge. It is in order to see whether this process has really come to an end, and above all to see whether, beyond statements of principles and declarations of good intentions, we are ready to accept the theoretical and practical consequences of theological pluralism, whether we have understood that all true evangelisation supposes the translation of the message which is to be transmitted, and by translation is here meant a presentation made in such a way that the meaning of the message may be received and understood, can be assimilated by those to whom it is addressed, and may ultimately be interpreted by them in the process of developing their own theology, and in order that they may construct their own Church. Here I should like to point out how necessary it is to rethink everything that has been said about the theandric nature of the Church: this is an analysis which can too easily languish where one is used to seeing the visible and hierarchical Church in full operation, but which becomes urgent and indispensable when we are faced with the almost superhuman task of establishing and *creating locally* that same Church, and supplying it with all its organs of function. It is easy to become critical or to wax ironic about the suggestion of an African or an Asiatic theology. But do people sufficiently realise that all forms of evangelisation require *not* the imposition of a certain form of discourse or model, but the transmission of a message which gives meaning and value to all people's lives, whatever the cultural world in question? It is on this condition, and on this condition alone, that evangelisation can become a humanising factor: that is, a factor of development, of cultural renewal, of ensoulment and conscientisation—in short, of salvation.

That, it seems to me, is the real problem. A nation dies at the level of its culture, and it is there that it lies fallow throughout centuries, or is reborn. And it is at the cultural level, that is at the level of a nation's interpretation of the world, that the question of development and of salvation is posed.

In the Church this movement of re-identification and liberation of nations, which are rediscovering themselves as peoples and also rediscovering their own uniqueness, has first of all to be acknowledged. It supposes that justice has been done to the will of peoples to build themselves in society as they wish, to construct themselves in the Church in accordance with their traditions and their own genius (*Ad Gentes*, § 22). At the World Synod of Bishops of 1974, held on the theme of evangelisation in the modern world, this claim was expressed with striking depth. It is the whole problem of the individual churches clearly posed at the level of the universal Church. But, in order to pose it properly, the Church should ask the forgiveness of the nations which it evangelised for certain restrictions of viewpoint, certain examples of Eurocentric triumphalism and certain associations with secular interests.

Vatican II asks us to renew our understanding of the nature of the Church. Its central affirmation was that of an authentic catholicity. The Church, the Council affirms, is *one and diverse*. It is not diverse for want of anything better but by reason of its very nature and mission. The Church of Jesus Christ was built on the basis of a number of local churches. 'These are, within the bosom of the communion of the Church, individual churches which rejoice in their own traditions without prejudice to the primacy of the

E

chair of Peter, which presides over the universal assembly of love, guarantees legitimate differences and ensures that, far from prejudicing unity, individual characteristics will on the contrary prove profitable. Hence, between the various parts of the Church, there are links of intimate communion in spiritual riches. The members of the people of God are called in effect to share their goods, and the words of the apostle apply to each of the churches: '. . . let each one place in the service of others the gift which he has received, like a good steward dispensing the grace of God in its varied forms' (1 Pet. 4:10) (*Lumen Gentium*, § 13).

It is essential to safeguard our otherness or identity without harming the revealed message. Only a hermeneutical process can make that possible. We cannot talk meaningfully of the significance of God in another culture unless we ourselves have entered into our own culture. *Nobody speaks from nowhere.* The experience of encountering another religion is possible only by means of tradition understood as a language. Hermeneutics therefore becomes dialogue to the extent to which one stays oneself on the ground of one's tradition, and to the extent to which one acknowledges one's own historical consciousness. This is an important finding. Christian religious language appeared within a pre-existing religious language which it assumed, fulfilled and transfigured. In other words, the human and religious experience of peoples constitutes the privileged location from the basis of which Christ may be encountered and recognised.

The result of the foregoing for the Christian mission is that it cannot, as in the past, start from the abstractly affirmed universality of Christianity, but from its particularity. Abstract consideration of Christianity as a universal religion leads easily to imperialism. Christianity considered as a religion alongside other religions forces us to think of God not as a given inscribed in a single tradition, which is exclusive, intolerant and victorious, but as an *eschatological problem* of the meeting of cultures in their ineradicable diversity. We discover God in the meetings which he encourages. 'I was a stranger and you took me in' (Matt. 25:35). Yes, 'God always reveals himself by tearing down the signs which nevertheless, like the veil of the Temple in the past, already indicate his coming. He bestows himself only in the tensions and in the building up of a human community', writes Certeau.[13] And his countenance will be unveiled fully only on the last day. Hurbon explains and amplifies thus: 'Confronted with a culture of the African, Asiatic or Afro-American type, Christianity is presented *a priori* as a universal culture and religion, and refuses to acknowledge the special nature of its language. It is on the basis of this individuality that its mission to other cultures is to be inaugurated. More precisely, all missions are first of all confrontations with cultures. Every announcement of the coming of the kingdom is located at the very point of the confrontation of different cultures.'[14]

These considerations (which unfortunately I cannot develop any further in the present space) start from the conviction that the Church is not identical with the kingdom of God. In other terms, the Church does not possess Jesus Christ or eternal salvation. Essentially, the term 'salvation' is synonymous with 'kingdom'; that is, it expresses the presence of the Saviour God acting through Christ in the cosmos and in all ages of history, and in particular in the mystery of each man who desires it. The reason is that God works for man's salvation in the very effort which man makes to save himself. We may say therefore that the kingdom is in principle co-extensive with the world of men and of human history. It allies itself with destiny in order to lead it to its conclusion. The action of evangelisation takes effect within the turns and ups-and-downs of history.[15] Given this, the kingdom is nothing other than the world converted to the Spirit of Christ. It is therefore far from setting itself against the world, just as it is far from allowing itself to be absorbed into the world. Nor is it inclined to withdraw or to set itself up fatally in a parallel history.

I bring together here the perspectives opened up by the Second Vatican Council. *Gaudium et Spes* locates the Church in the midst of the world—not over against it. It is the problems of the men of our time which interest the Christian and the Church. The Church does not claim, with the gravity of a universally accepted authority, to offer a ready made solution, but accepts the fact that it has to search along with all men of good will, in accordance with John XXIII's apt formula, consenting not only to learn from specialists the technical details of these problems, but to apply together with all those who reflect on the nature and problems of our own times, the reflection which is inspired by the gospel of Jesus Christ.

The increasingly vital realisation that the world itself is a divine sacrament is certainly capable of broadening the perspectives opened up by the Second Vatican Council. Would it be wrong to see the other religions as sacraments of the different aspects of the kingdom? The world is becoming increasingly secularised, as is the Church. It will probably have to act in the future world more like the leaven in the dough than like the fortress on the mountain. And when the world is quite clearly manifest as the sacrament of God, the rôle of the Church (in its historical form) and of all the other religions will have come to an end. The world itself will be the Church: that is, the authentic people of God, according to the wholly filial dignity of its members, definitively established for and in Christ.

Therefore we have to ask basic questions about the rôle of the Church—the small band of Christ's followers which day by day is becoming a minority. How can it be the place in which other religions and cultures find their fulfilment in Christ? In what way are they oriented towards it? (*Lumen Gentium*, § 16). In order to reach their fulfilment in Christ, must the other religions die and be reborn in Christ, or must the local church also dive into the sea of these religions and emerge shining in its messianic rôle, like its divine Founder when he was baptised by the Forerunner?

It is on the basis of the foregoing that it is possible to understand the Church's mission to all men, which is no accidental feature of Christianity, but arises from its eschatological hope. For Vatican II, the missionary responsibility of the Church consists precisely in restoring the values of the other religions to Christ, the Founder of all values. It will be perfectly achieved at the end of time (*Ad Gentes*, § 9). If the Church is moving towards a fulfilment at the end of time (*Lumen Gentium*, § 5), may we say that the other religions are to find their fulfilment in Christ, within the kingdom, at the end of time? Are we to speak then of a mutual fulfilment, a mutual conversion, a mutual complement, which will lead all the religions, including Christianity, towards their fulfilment in the total Christ, who is the eschatological kingdom? Or as Teilhard de Chardin said, in regard to the Buddhists and Confucians, surely it is possible for us to enrich our spirit to some degree from the rich sap which is circulating in their veins and at the same time to offer them the means of invigorating it? Surely we can try to complete ourselves in the process of converting them?

Here I align myself with the viewpoint of Professor Mbiti, who states explicitly: 'Christianity has spoken too long and too much. Perhaps it has not listened enough. For too long a time it has passed judgment on other cultures, other religions and other societies, while keeping itself aloof from all criticism. Perhaps the time has now come for western Christianity to be more humble in its approach to other religions and cultures, if it wishes to have some effect here in Africa. Christianity should first of all confront this traditional fund with an open spirit, with the readiness to change it and to be changed by it. In particular, I ask my brothers from Europe and America to allow us to do what, in their judgment, may be considered as erroneous. Allow us to wreak havoc, as it were, upon Christianity in our continent, just as you have done in Europe and America—to put it politely. When we write on particular aspects of Christianity or other academic matters, no one should expect us to use the vocabulary and approach employed in

Europe and in America. Allow us to say certain things in our own way, whether we make mistakes or not. Here we are mainly facing the problems of transmitting the unchanging gospel as effectively as possible.'[16]

The above are, in summary form, a few questions which occurred to me when considering the general theme of this issue. After all, I thought, after centuries of separations between Christian theology and non-western cultures, perhaps it is too early to unite the two in an authentic way and without practising a dual form of purification—of western scientific culture, which always brings into play unconscious negative postulates, and of the Christian theologies which are imprisoned in superannuated formulas and methods. We have to agree that this task will still take a long time. I believe in the strength of patience and expectation. I know that there are now many Third World theologians who have vowed in silence to prepare favourable conditions for a new universe of thought in which Christian faith and human intelligence will meet. They are working, like bridge-builders, to join divided arches.[17]

Translated by J. Cumming

Notes

1. Declaration of the bishops of Africa and Madagascar: '*Promouvoir* l'evangélisation dans la corresponsabilité in *La documentation Catholique* No. 1664 (1974) 995.

2. *Ibid.*

3. Quoted by Cardinal P. Zoungrana in *Bulletin de Théologie Africaine* 2 No. 4 142.

4. *Collection Culture et Religions, Présence Africaine* (1976) 174 pages.

5. Louvain (1977), 796 pages.

6. *Collection Le Sycomore* (Namur-Paris 1979) I, 347 pages, II, 245 pages.

7. In *Concilium* 135 (1980) vii.

8. See on this point a pertinent work, E. Poulat *Histoire, dogme et critique dans le crise moderniste* (Paris 1962). For more immediate information, see C. Tresmontant *La Crise moderniste* (Paris 1979).

9. Cardinal Malula *L'Evèque africain hier et aujourd'hui* (Kinshasa 1980).

10. O. Bimwenyi Kweshi 'Inculturation en Afrique et attitude des agents de l'évangelisation' in *Bulletin de Théologie Africaine* 3 No. 5 6-7.

11. E. Dussel *Histoire et théologie de la Libération* (Paris 1974) pp. 71-72.

12. See *La Reconnaissance des différences, chemin de la solidarité.* The second conference of Africans and Europeans organised by the Société Africaine de Culture et Terre Entière with the collaboration of the Amis italiens de Présence Africaine (Brazzaville, 21-26 February 1974, Paris 1973). See also *Civilisation noire et Eglise Catholique*, the Abidjan Colloquium, 12-17 September 1977, *Présence Africaine* (Paris 1978).

13. M. de Certeau *L'Étranger ou l'union dans la différence* (Paris 1969) p. 224.

14. L. Hurbon *Dieu dans le vaudou haïtien* (Paris 1972) pp. 239-240.

15. If there is a 'universal revelation' exceeding the Judaeo-Christian historical revelation, there is also a Word of God which is directed outside the Church and a salvation which is accessible by non-ecclesiastical religious means, and even through 'secular' forms of mediation which are as various as human ideals. The Church welcomes and is ready to respect all human values; they are 'a preparation for the gospel' (*Lumen Gentium*, § 16).

16. Quoted by R. de Haes 'La Théologie des réligions après Vatican II' in *La Pertinence du Christianisme en Afrique*. Sixth Theological Encounter organised by the Catholic Theological Faculty of Kinshasa, Zaïre (1972) p. 437.

17. This conviction was behind the founding in 1976 of the Ecumenical Association of Third World Theologians. See O. Bimwenyi Kweshi 'Déplacements. A l'origine de l'Association Oecuménique de Théologiens du Tiers-Monde' in *Bulletin de Théologie Africaine* 2 No. 3 41-53. The publications of this association are certainly of importance in the history of modern theology. See especially C. Abesamis *et al. Théologiens du Tiers-Monde. Du conformisme à l'indépendance.* The Dar-Es-Salaam colloquium and its extensions (Paris 1978) 267 pages; Kofi Appiah-Kubi *et al. Libération ou adaptation? La théologie africaine s'interroge.* The Accra colloquium (Paris 1979) 235 pages; Virginia Fabella *Asia's Struggle for Full Humanity: Towards a Relevant Theological Conference* (New York 1979) 202 pages.

Kari Elisabeth Børresen

Women and Men in the Creation Narratives and in the Church

IN NORWAY, Roman Catholics are a very small minority: in 1978, out of a total population of just over four million, they numbered about thirteen thousand. As for Norwegian society, it is not, or rather is no longer, patriarchal,[1] and the Roman Catholic Church, being a missionary church, does not emphasise aspects of Catholic doctrine which would conflict with this social background. It lays little stress, for example, on the subordinate place of women, a legacy of traditional patristic and scholastic theology that still survives in the institutional Church.

I was already ten when my mother became a Catholic, and that at a time when conversions were few, but many of those which did take place involved members of the intellectual and social élite; my childhood socialisation was therefore not of the patriarchal type which is very common among girls from traditional Catholic milieux. So when I went to France in 1951, it was a cultural shock to find myself among women who had what appeared to me to be a negative image of themselves. I gradually came to realise that their attitude was a result of the basically male-centred, androcentric teaching and institutions of the Roman Catholic Church.

In 1961, in order to throw some light on this teaching and its influence, I began research into theological anthropology. This was before Vatican II, and well before 'women's studies' and 'feminist theology' came into fashion.[2]

My purpose in giving this sketch of my personal history is to show that I am typical neither of socially integrated women from 'Catholic' countries, nor of women who have a patriarchal background but have broken free of it. The latter often remain scarred both by their conformist education and by their break away from it, whereas, coming from Scandinavia, I was in the privileged position of being able to approach theological androcentrism as something foreign and external to myself, and that, I believe, enables me to see it in a different and more detached light.

The present situation

In western Europe and North America, that is, in those parts of the world that share what can be called North Atlantic civilisation, women have for the last few decades had equality with men—both in theory and to a large extent in practice—in the fields of law, economics and physiology. This emancipation from the patriarchal structures that characterise all societies known to history was made possible, in my view, by what I call the biological revolution. This revolution, perhaps the most important in all human history, was brought about by the *artificial* interventions of medicine, which have altered the old *natural* balance between fertility and mortality. Infant mortality has been almost eradicated, and child-bearing can now be controlled by effective means of contraception. The conjunction of these two factors means that women are no longer worn out physically and mentally by their child-bearing rôle, but have energy to spare for activities outside the family. Their rôle as mothers is now just one part of their lives, along with their career. It goes without saying that patriarchal societies saw procreation as woman's *raison d'être* and, in the education of girls, laid strong emphasis on their future rôle as mothers, because of the physiological realities of life at that time. Before the biological revolution, societies with a high infant mortality rate depended on the reproductive capacity of women for their very survival. Even if there was overpopulation in relation to the available resources, the reproductive potential was controlled by infanticide, particularly of new-born girls, since the known abortifacients and means of contraception were unreliable. So the actual number of pregnancies did not decrease significantly; in other words, the system used to control population increase did not leave women with energy to spare.

The modern women's liberation movement seems to me therefore to be a result of the biological revolution. Any struggle for liberation presupposes that there is a surplus of energy available to be used creatively; and any liberation of women depends unconditionally on effective contraception. Unless she can control her own fertility and bear children *as and when she chooses*, no woman can organise her family and professional life freely. Quite obviously, this kind of freedom of choice is totally irreconcilable with a patriarchal system in which women are seen as the property of their husbands, with the latter controlling the woman's reproductive capacity.

1. WOMEN AND MEN IN THE CREATION NARRATIVES

The classical synthesis

The classical teaching on the relation between woman and man is based on the creation stories in Genesis 1:26-27 and 2:7, 18-24. The two chapters, it should be noted, were treated as one narrative.[3] It takes no training in exegesis to see that the first text states clearly that the man and the women were created in God's image, whereas the second text gives pride of place to the creation of Adam. Late Judaic commentators interpreted Genesis 1:26-27 in the light of Genesis 2:7, which was seen as giving primacy to Adam. The creation of Eve as told in Genesis 2:18-24 was taken to imply a hierarchical relation between the two sexes: the woman was created *from* man, and so was materially dependent on him, and *for* man, and therefore was existentially dependent on him. Only the human male was thought to be made in the image of God; the female was not so made. There is an example of this type of rabbinical exegesis in 1 Cor. 11:7: 'A man has no need to cover his head, because man is the image of God, and the mirror of his glory, whereas woman reflects the glory of man.'[4]

Any discourse about God and his relation to mankind, and so theology in the strict sense of the term, is necessarily the product of human experience at a particular historical moment, and is therefore socially and culturally conditioned. Scripture itself and the Judaeo-Christian interpretation of it have a common socio-cultural background, which was patriarchal. So just as the human male was made in God's image, God was spoken of in male, andromorphic metaphors such as king, judge, patriarch-husband, and father.[5] Classical Christian teaching retained these androcentric formulations which present God andromorphously.

The Fathers of the Church subordinated the interpretation given in 1 Cor. 11:7 to Genesis 1:26-27. To resolve the difficulty caused by the literal contradiction between the two texts, they fell back on the allegorical method of exegesis used by Philo of Alexandria (born between 15 and 10 BC). In his interpretation of Genesis 2:7 and 18-24 and Genesis 1:26-27 taken together, Philo distinguished between two functions of the human soul: the higher function represented man, and the lower one, woman.[6] [7]

Augustine combined this allegorical interpretation with a dualistic definition of human beings. For him, sexual differences only concerned the body; the soul was the same in both man and women, being asexual because it was spiritual. The image of God was only in the rational soul, which Augustine, following a patristic presupposition derived from Platonist anthropology, contrasted with the sexually differentiated body. From this it clearly followed that woman, like man, was made in the image of God. Nevertheless, because she was created *for* man and in so far as she was sexually differentiated from him, woman could not represent the perfection of that image. So as a human being she was made in God's image but as a woman she was not. Discussing the point that the bodily difference between man and women is a figure of the differences in function within the human soul, itself created in the image of God, Augustine writes: 'A woman together with her husband is an image of God, so that the whole of this human substance forms just one image (Genesis 1:26-27); but when she is considered as man's helpmeet (Genesis 2:18), which is what is specific to her as a woman, she is not an image of God (1 Cor. 11:7). Man on the other hand, in what is specific to him, is an image of God, an image of God that is as perfect and entire as when woman is linked with him to form one with him.'[7]

Despite this spiritualistic interpretation of the image of God, which takes account only of the asexual soul, classical teaching considers the male sex as made in God's image in a normative sense.[8] There is therefore a split between the human and the female which, on this androcentric view, does not exist between the human and the male. The male is the standard human being, the norm; the female is defined only by the way she differs from this norm.

The classical teaching thus keeps to the hierarchical interpretation of Genesis 2:7 and 18-24. Woman, in so far as she is sexually differentiated from man, exists for *one* purpose only: to fulfil her rôle, the subordinate rôle, in procreation.[9] Just as there is a split between the female and the human, so there is a difference between her finality as a woman and her finality as an asexual being made in God's image. She is subordinate in the order of creation because she is female, but in the order of salvation, being in the image of God, she has the same value as man.[10]

Contemporary teaching

Contemporary theological anthropology no longer questions whether woman was created in God's image; Genesis 1:26-27 is taken literally, regardless of the difficulties this causes for the interpretation of 1 Cor. 11:7. The dualistic definition of the human being which classical teaching made use of has also been abandoned. The specific characteristics of the male are no longer considered to be supra-sexual; the whole human being, man or woman, is seen as the image of God. Genesis 2:18-24 is not now taken as implying that Eve was existentially dependent on Adam. But despite all these changes, the idea that women exist only to produce offspring still persists, though in less clear-cut form than before.

It must be noted too that the term 'complementarity' is used with a frequency such that it lays strong stress on the non-interchangeability of women's and men's rôles in society. This amounts to defining specifically feminine or masculine functions in a way that simply follows through from the classical view of woman as an auxiliary necessary for procreation. The subordinate aspect of woman's rôle is not emphasised, at least in the theory, because it is incompatible with the socio-cultural circumstances of North Atlantic civilisation, but this merely highlights the fact that modern theological anthropology is inconsistent: it has abandoned the old androcentric premises but retains the conclusions drawn from them.

This illogicality is particularly marked in Christology and ecclesiology, and the following key example illustrates it perfectly. Patristic typology made Christ the new Adam and the Church the new Eve, following scriptural indications (see Hos. 2:19-20; 2 Cor. 11:2; Eph. 5:32); here, the hierarchy between the sexes is transposed from the order of creation to the order of salvation, since the male element represents the divine partner and the female element the human partner. Androcentrism is set alongside theocentrism. The whole analogy is based on the subordination of woman to man which is self-evident in a patriarchal society. The hierarchical relation between Adam and Eve, and therefore between men and women in general, is used to represent the ontological hierarchy between God and creation. But without the presupposition that woman is inferior to man, the symbolism loses all meaning.

Outlook for the future

In the past, the androcentrism of the scriptural texts and the androcentrism of classical exegesis reinforced each other, but their alliance is now being shattered. The collapse of the patriarchal structures which underpinned it means that there will have to be nothing short of a revolution in every aspect of human talk about God, a Copernican revolution, to meet a challenge more radical than any that Christian doctrines have had to face before. It will spread to the whole of theology, and will affect both the concept of God and theological anthropology, both Christology and ecclesiology. It will transform not only the linguistic expression of ideas about the divine, but also their expression in symbols. Like any other set of symbols, Christian symbolism developed against a specific socio-cultural background, which in this case was androcentric. When the social background changes, as it is doing today, existing symbols cease to be meaningful, and new ones have to be invented.

Let us take the notion of God as an example. If the image of God is found in woman as well as in man, then both female and male metaphors will have to be used to speak of God. If both woman and man are made in God's image, God will have to be spoken of in anthropomorphic terms, not just in andromorphic ones. Obviously, no human terms can adequately represent the transcendence of God, but a combination of the two types of metaphor can show the totality of the divine since it is based on the totality of the human.[11] The ontological relation between God and mankind can no longer be properly illustrated by nuptial imagery, which rests on an androcentric use of the incarnation, i.e., God became man in the normative sex (*homo factus est = vir factus est*). Outside a patriarchal society it becomes meaningless and therefore incomprehensible to transpose this sexual hierarchy into the order of salvation by giving Christ a symbolically male rôle in relation to the Church, his symbolically subordinate spouse. To go on propagating this kind of symbolism would be harmful, since it would be legitimating the androcentric structures of the Church.

2. WOMEN AND MEN IN THE CHURCH

Right up to our own day, the Roman Catholic Church has always encouraged the subordination of women both in society at large and within the Church itself. But the development of North Atlantic societies away from patriarchal structures has forced the

Church to adapt itself to the changing times, and since Vatican II it has frequently stated the principle of the equivalence of men and women in society. But it should be noted that statements of this kind are always accompanied by reservations, based on what is termed the complementarity of the sexes, for they talk of specifically female rôles. In other words, though the classical pattern of hierarchy between the sexes has been abandoned, the division of rôles based on an individual's sex is still clearly retained.[12]

In any case, the duly affirmed equivalence of the sexes does not operate within the institutional Church. Since women are excluded from the ordained ministries, they are automatically excluded from any jurisdictional power in the Church. In that, they are in the same position as non-ordained men, but the inferior position of women even within the laity can be seen in the strongly androcentric 1917 Code of Canon Law, now being revised.

There are two papal documents, both later than Vatican II, which show the persistence of androcentrism. One treats the order of creation, while the other applies it to the order of salvation. Both are striking examples of the muddled thinking involved in retaining a conclusion when the premises it is based on have been dropped; in this they are typically transitional. They are both attempts to deal with questions which have arisen out of the biological revolution and the consequent liberation of women.

The encyclical *Humanae Vitae* (1968) is innovatory in so far as it accepts in principle the control of human fertility. The traditional connection between sexual activity and procreation which was comprehensible before the biological revolution, and provided a natural frame of reference in classical moral theology, is now dropped. But the encyclical will not allow that effective means of contraception are legitimate, because they are 'artificial'; it thus goes against the principle of voluntary procreation which it has nevertheless accepted—and which, be it noted, it calls by the highly androcentric name of responsible fatherhood (*paternitas conscia*).[13]

The arguments in favour of the methods it terms 'natural' and which involve a form of continence—another androcentric term, since *continentia* connotes retention of semen—clearly derived from the Augustinian tradition wherein concupiscence, seen as evil, was neutralised by procreation, seen as good, while married love was expressed by sexual continence.[14]

The method of birth-control which consists in avoiding intercourse during ovulation is androcentric in so far as many women are more capable of orgasm at that time than during other stages of the menstrual cycle.[15] But of greater importance is the fact that the rejection of effective methods of birth-control means that women are refused the right to control their own reproductive function. In this sense, the encyclical *Humanae Vitae* sets itself against the liberation of women which the biological revolution has made possible. It helps to perpetuate the traditional dominance of the child-bearing rôle in a woman's life and the no less traditional division between masculine and feminine rôles in society.

The declaration *Inter insigniores* (1977) preserves a similar division between the rôles of the sexes within the Church, since it defines the ordained priesthood as a specifically male function. The arguments rest on patristic typology, with the rôle of Christ seen as male, and that of the Church as female. The lack of connection between premises and conclusion is patent: the declaration claims not to be arguing from the subordinate status of women, yet it invokes patristic and scholastic texts which presuppose it. The persistence of the idea that only male human beings are made in God's image should be noted: only a man can act *in persona Christi*, that is, can represent or figure Christ.[16] In other words, the declaration highlights the androcentricity of contemporary Christology and ecclesiology. The doctrine that men and women alike are made in the image of God is not yet being taken seriously in these central areas. The new meta-androcentric view will make it necessary to transcend the model in which the rôles of the sexes are fundamentally non-interchangeable and so to put forward totally new dogmatic formulations.

3. WHERE DOES THE CHURCH STAND NOW?

The stimulus of the biological revolution has provoked the Church into updating itself, but—like other ecclesial communities[17]—it is doing so slowly and reluctantly. Historically, it is the Church's ability to adapt to changing socio-cultural circumstances that has allowed it to survive for nearly 2,000 years. But these adaptations always take place with a time-lag, the institutions of the Church not being prophetic. Today, the collapse of patriarchal structures in North Atlantic civilisation has made the gap between the Church and the socio-cultural backgound wider than ever. As a result, many women are seeing the Church as an obstacle between Christ and themselves, and are asking a burning question: Is the liberation of women going to take place within the Church and with the Church, or outside it and against it?

Student and colleague friends of both sexes often ask me how it is possible for a woman who was not socialised on the patriarchal pattern to remain in the Roman Catholic Church. I try to reply by distinguishing between the institutional Church, with its massive androcentricity, and the Church as the instrument of salvation established by Christ. The physical realities of human incarnation mean that salvation has to work through our transitory human state; because of the human condition God has to reveal himself to us through human forms and language. This hermeneutic principle was well put by the German cardinal Nicolas of Cusa (1401-1464): Christ speaks to us humanly of God.[18] But 'humanly' means conditioned by a particular culture, which in the case of Christ was a patriarchal culture. The androcentricity of Scripture is a historical fact.

There are certainly some positive signs in Scripture, some texts that could be used to show a favourable attitude to women. But to inflate them for apologetic purposes would be to lack historical sense, quite apart from the recourse to Scripture alone it would presuppose. If our work is to put forward a constructive theological corrective, it must face up squarely to the problems posed by a patriarchal Scripture and tradition, and not minimise their seriousness.

God is continuously revealing himself in and by Christ in unity with the Holy Spirit and through the Church. This living revelation in time takes place and will of necessity continue to take place through the medium of human language in different cultures. If the cultural background ceases to be patriarchal, the language of revelation will no longer be androcentric, but will become human in the full sense of the term, both male and female.

I have myself no doubt that the liberation of women will come about in and with the Church, guided by the Spirit which gives life. It will spread first to the formulation of doctrine and theological symbolism, and then to the juridical and institutional facets of the Church.

The period of transition we are passing through is likely to be painful for the women and men who are aware how great the changes will have to be. Erasmus, who despite the state of the institutional Church in his day was so faithful to the Church as a saving reality, can offer us a watchword: 'I bear with this Church in the hope it will one day improve, and the Church will have to bear with me in the hope I will one day improve.'[19] So we must put up with the Church, so androcentric in its theology, its symbolism and its institutions, until it stops being an obstacle on the way to Christ and becomes in him the means of salvation. And the Church will have to put up with us—who may not be prophets but at least are not socialised on the patriarchal model—until we improve. The Holy Spirit is doubtless neither gynocentric nor androcentric; let us leave it the task of defining the necessary improvements.

Translated by Ruth Murphy

Notes

1. See *Norwegian Society* ed. N. R. Ramsey (Oslo, London and New York 1974).
2. See K. E. Børresen 'Male-Female, a Critique of Traditional Christian Theology' *Temenos* 13 (1977) 31-42 for an account of my research.
3. The hypothesis that the two texts had different sources was only put forward in 1711, by Henning Bernard Witter.
4. See J. S. Jervell *Imago Dei. Gen. I, 26 f—im Spätjudentum, in der Gnosis und in der paulinischen Briefen* (Göttingen 1960).
5. See P. Trible *God and the Rhetoric of Sexuality* (Philadelphia 1979) for the occasional use of feminine metaphors in the OT.
6. See R. A. Baer *Philo's Use of the Categories Male and Female* (Leiden 1970).
7. *De Trinitate* XII, 7, 10. See also *De Genesi ad litteram*, III, 22, 34.
8. See Aquinas' interpretation of 1 Cor. 11:7 in *Summa Theologiae*, T. Gilby, OP, ed. (London and New York 1964-1976) XIII, 1a, 93, 4 ad 1: 'But as regards a secondary point, God's image is found in man in a way in which it is not found in woman; for man is the beginning and end of woman, just as God is the beginning and end of all creation.'
9. Augustine puts it thus in *De Genesi ad litteram* IX, 5, 9: 'If woman was not given as a helpmeet to man in order to bear his children, in what way could she be a help to him? . . . For living and conversing together, how preferable the companionship of two male friends is to that of a man and a woman!'
10. See K. E. Børresen *Subordination et Equivalence. Nature et rôle de la femme d'après Augustin et Thomas d'Aquin* (Oslo and Paris 1968). For a summary, see my article 'Fondements anthropologiques de la relation entre l'homme et la femme dans la théologie classique' *Concilium* 12 (1976) 27-39. (This is a reference to the French language edition. The article is not available in English, since only four issues of the English language editon were published in 1975 and 1976, and Vol. 100 1976, which was devoted to 'Sexuality in Contemporary Catholicism', did not include the author's article: English Language Editor's note.)
11. See K. E. Børresen 'Christ notre mère, la théologie de Julienne de Norwich' *Mitteilungen und Forschungsbeiträge der Cusanus-Gesellschaft* 13 (1978) 320-329.
12. See *Gaudium et Spes* § 9, § 29 and § 60. Paul VI, Apostolic letter *Octogesima adveniens* 13, *AAS* 63 (1971) pp. 410-411. Paul VI, Address to the members of the Pontifical Commission on Women, *AAS* 68 (1976) pp. 197-201. Speech by Mgr P. J. Cordes, the leader of the Holy See's delegation to the UN Women's Decade world conference, *Osservatore Romano* weekly ed. 33 (12-8-1980) p. 14: 'It is therefore quite clear that woman as such is an image of God and a reflection of the divine perfection. To develop her personality fully, she must fulfil herself as a woman. Her model must be God alone, not the human male, because she is made in God's image.' (Note that woman is made in God's image, and God is correspondingly not seen andromorphically; but specifically feminine and masculine rôles remain.)
13. *Humanae Vitae* II, 10, *AAS* 60 (1968) p. 487.
14. Augustine speaks of 'bene uti malo'; see *De bono conjugali* III, 3 and *De conjugiis adulterinis* II, 12. He is opposed to the method of contraception the Manicheans use, i.e., avoiding the female fertile period: see *De moribus ecclesiae Catholicae et de moribus Manichaeorum* II, 18,

65; *Contra Faustum Manichaeum* XV, 7. For the expression of love by continence, see *De sermone Domini in monte* I, XV, 41-42.

15. See R. C. Friedman, S. W. Hurt, M. S. Arnoff 'Behaviour and the Menstrual Cycle' *Signs* 5 (1980) 727-728.

16. *Inter insigniores* V, *AAS* 69 (1977) p. 109.

17. See the Norwegian Act of Parliament on Equal Status between the Sexes, No. 45 of 9 June 1978, para. 2. The Act concerns discrimination between women and men in all areas, with the exception of internal conditions in religious communities.

18. Nicolas of Cusa *De principio, Philosophisch-theologische Schriften* II (Vienna 1966) p. 288. And see *Dialogus de Genesi, Opera omnia* IV (Hamburg 1959) p. 114.

19. Erasmus *Hyperaspites* I, *Ausgewählte Schriften* 4 (Darmstadt 1969) p. 248.

Frei Betto

Social De-personalisation
and Prayer

THE PHENOMENON of social de-personalisation is characterised by the swamping of human individuality in the generic nature of the 'mass', the collectivity. It is typical of societies in an advanced stage of technological development. Here, I am not going to examine its occurrence in the Socialist countries, but concentrate on its structural causes and its relationship with the life of prayer in the 'Christian' countries whose people live under the capitalist system, especially in Latin America.

1. THE STRUCTURAL CAUSES OF SOCIAL DE-PERSONALISATION

The pragmatic philosophy of capitalism defends the freedom of the individual in so far as it is directly related to private property and capital. The owners of the means of production, as a class, have the 'right' to protect their profits, enshrined in structures and laws of the bourgeois State. Competition, the competitive spirit, the struggle to win markets, become values basic to human achievement—notwithstanding the fact that the dominant theory tries to hide these selfish 'values' under the universal guise of individual freedom.

The majority of the population of Latin America is reduced to the basic functions of production and consumption. People live their existence as a mere *biological process*, with survival the immediate concern, not as a *biographical process*, involving conscious appreciation and historic understanding of the meaning of existence. Work is elevated to be a basic value, even in ecclesiastical pronouncements, as though it were something divorced from relationships of property. Now capitalism deprives the majority of the population of ownership of capital, of the means of production, of the tools and the fruits of work. The worker is not himself the subject of his own existence: he is dependent on fluctuations in the labour market brought about by political or economic considerations. All the operative has is the strength of his hands—a merchandise for which the owner can pay with a wage that does not correspond to its true value. The capitalist earns his profit from the difference—the value added.

In order to justify the system of exploitation, and at the same time reinforce it, those who own the money control the means of de-personalisation: the mass media—TV, radio, cinema, record companies, newspapers and magazines. Through these they impose habits and customs that make consumerism a supreme value in social life. People are socially fulfilled to the extent that they possess the goods that symbolise human well-being and happiness.

Social de-personalisation invades human subjectivity: the consumerist cycle requires a permanent changing of habits, customs and values. Personal choice suffers an accelerated process of outdating. As the vehicle of market proposals and offers, publicity manipulates the sensitive areas of personal desires, exciting them with a whirlwind of images, symbols and meanings. Exposed to the glamour of the system, people's own inner identity is threatened. The system is concerned to reduce the individual to his producing and consuming 'outer self'. Caught up in the oracles of the dominant ideology, de-personalised into mere producer-consumers, Christians feel threatened in their spiritual lives.

2. THE UNIVERSALITY OF URBAN SOCIETY

Among Christians, prayer is still associated with a rural, pre-modern nostalgia, redolent of the solitude of the fields and the silence of regions beyond the reach of the electronic age. Popular images encouraging personal and intimate encounter with the Father would be lonely woods, silent oceans or pine-clad mountains, images of our deep-seated desire to recover the peace lost under the pressure of the means of social de-personalisation. This reaction is rooted in our inability to find a life of prayer in a modern urban setting. So there is still a strong quest for prayer involving 'flight' from the city—which is where, when all is said and done, the existence of modern man is decided.

The city is present even in rural areas through the mass media. Electronic societies universalise urbanisation, and the city becomes little more than a geographical point. TV, radio, the telephone and the motor car have abolished the distinction between the city and the country. The solitude propitious to prayer hardly exists even in the hills and woods any more.

How does one pray in a de-personalising society? We have to find out how to preserve and enlarge our praying 'inner self' in a society whose means of ideological diffusion invade our subjectivity and accentuate the contradiction between our essence (as sons of God) and our existence (as victims of capitalist oppression).

3. A NEW SETTING FOR THEOPHANY

We cannot hide the existence of technological advance, urban development and social de-personalisation. We need to know what produces them and where they are leading. It is worse than useless to create imaginary structures as though we were living in the Spain of St Teresa or the France of St Thérèse of Lisieux. Even though some religious might enjoy the sanctuary of impenetrable cloisters, the crucial point is the conditions for making prayer possible in the daily lives of the great mass of the faithful. All are called equally to communion with the Father. How are they to achieve it in a de-personalising society?

If we see prayer as an initiative taken by the Spirit in our lives (and not as mere religious technique capable of providing religious 'experiences'), we need to find out where the Father is speaking to us today. Are we going to find him in the depths of the forests, the silence of the prairies or the centre of the earth? Is the lack of God in our lives brought about by him, or by us refusing to see a new theophanic setting? Elijah waited for Yahweh to show himself in a mighty wind, an earthquake and a fire (1 Kings 19:11-12). But Yahweh was not in any of these, but in the gentle breeze that came after them. Elijah had a hard road to follow in order to discover the new setting for theophany.

In Latin America, the setting for the new theophany will not be a geographical one (woods or mountains), but a social one: the place of the oppressed (Matt. 25:31-46). There can be no prayer that takes us away from the people to reach God, no dualism separating Christian practice, based on charity, from the practice of prayer. In the Bible, conversion to God is directly associated with the decision to bring justice to the oppressed (Jer. 22:13-16; 31:34; Isa. 5:7; 6:4-6; 58:6-7; Amos 7:10 ff; 1 John 4:19-21). We open ourselves to the loving presence of the Father by listening to the clamour of the poor. Conversion is not a new way of feeling; it is a new way of acting. Fired by the preaching of John the Baptist, the people asked: 'What must we *do*?' (Luke 3:10). Acceptance in faith presupposes a decision to go out of ourselves in love (1 Cor. 13:2) and to eradicate existing inequalities: 'He who has two coats, let him share with him who has none; and he who has food, let him do likewise' (Luke 3:11).

Praying from the basis of the social setting of the poor and their need for liberation is placing subjectivity at the opposite pole from the instruments of social de-personalisation. The organic commitment (Gramsci) to the cause of the oppressed neutralises, in us, the proposals that try to reduce us to producers-consumers. In this meeting with our marginalised neighbours, we meet ourselves anew. There is God (Matt. 25:31-46). God is not silent where the community hears the words of the oppressed. This is why there has never been any discussion of 'the death of God' in Latin America, where, in recent years, the Church has identified itself with the process of liberating the masses subjected to a dependent, peripheral and exclusive capitalism, whose beneficiaries amount to a mere 5 per cent of the population. In the signs of liberation, Christians recognise the presence of God—who, in the gospels, can hardly be perceived in subjective phenomena or private experiences (i.e., that *privatisation* of faith which is not properly evangelical, but rather a legacy of pagan mysticism, hostile or indifferent to the outside world). When John the Baptist sent his disciples to ask Jesus: 'Are you he who is to come, or shall we look for another?' (Luke 7:20), the reply was based on specific facts showing the transformation of reality, the new order emerging from its opposite: 'Go and tell John what you have seen and heard: the blind receive their sight, the lame walk, lepers are cleansed, and the deaf hear, the dead are raised up, the poor have good news preached to them . . .' (Luke 7:22).

In a de-personalising society, where the ecclesial community itself runs the risk of being seen as one more institution belonging to the civil power (a cultural, charitable, scholastic institution), it is among the poor that the Church will rediscover its true identity. Only by inserting itself in the opposite side to the consumer society—the social setting of the oppressed—can the ecclesial community free itself from being absorbed by the ruling structures and legitimising or sacralising them

4. THE UNITY BETWEEN PRAYER AND ACTION

Christian prayer encourages the unity between knowing in faith and experiencing in love—essence and existence. Through prayer, we impress an evangelical character on our actions and increase our faith. Praying breaks our resistance to love, sharpens our evangelical sensitivity so as to make the life of Christ present in our lives. Prayer makes us see reality through the eyes of God. It is the place *par excellence* where, in the Spirit that inspires it, we reach the fullness of our freedom in relation to other people, objects and the world.

Faith, nourished by prayer, enables us to break for ever from the harmful elements introduced into our lives by the ideology supporting the de-personalising society. It frees us from sin, from a reifying attitude, and enlarges the space in us available to the transforming action of grace. It makes us undertake a new reading of the historical process, through which we can see its ultimate and absolute meaning, without the danger of absolutising the data of a partial, immediate, rationalistic or 'scientific' reading, as the means of communication propose.

Perception of these harmful elements, which stem from the historical structure of sin, will develop as we engage ourselves in a liberating praxis capable of passing judgment on our personal and community prayer. In this way, prayer will not lend itself to the alienating rôle of trying to reconcile, on the level of conscience, social—and even personal—antagonisms which can, in fact, only be reconciled on the level of reality. It does not hide reality, but uncovers it.

All prayer has an ideological content. There is no such thing as 'chemically' pure, distilled prayer, prayer that will act like a biological washing powder. It is not a question of stripping prayer of its cultural mediations and expressions, but of recognising the ideological source from which it springs: the entrenched proposals of the ruling powers, perhaps, whose products stultify our faith and distort our vision of reality, or an alliance with the popular classes, opening up a furrow of hope in the ground of history, through which can flow the river leading to the Promise? This conjunction—between the definitive data of Christian revelation (which integrate the content of our faith) and the historical moment when these same data take effective shape—should be brought about by the mediation of an ideology contrary to the dominant one, a just ideology reflecting the aspirations of the poor to justice. The devout old lady who spends her days on her knees may not automatically reach this conjunction or this break with the dominant ideology. Her union with God is real—but it holds an alienating discontinuity if she ignores the disunity among people or imagines that social differences can be resolved in the psychological sphere of good intentions or through the miraculous action of divine power summoned by our intercessions. . . .

5. THE POLITICAL DIMENSION OF PRAYER

Christian prayer involves a deep criticism of de-personalising society, in so far as it arises from the social setting of those who are the negation of that society and, at the same time, the ideal setting of theophany—the poor. In this way, the political dimension of prayer links the purpose of union with God to that of union among the people. Christian prayer has the basic objective: 'That they may all be one' (John 17:21). There is no other way besides this quest for reconciliation which the Spirit puts into our hearts so that it can then take concrete form in the political project, the building of a more just society under future régimes and systems—imperfect stages on the road of progressive liberation which only the final manifestation of the kingdom will bring to full fruition.

We can feel delicious inner spiritual 'comforts' without sharing the anxieties of those who hunger and thirst after justice; we can feel a great uplift of the spirit and enjoy ecstasies and visions without the least awareness of the contradictions (disunities) between the social classes. But these are not the forms of prayer the gospel teaches us and the spirituality of liberation requires of us. Christian prayer is neither flight, consolation, delight nor opium. It cannot be narcissistically enjoyed by our inner senses or for the pleasure it affords our egos. It associates recognition of the holiness of God with the supplication that is at once promise and project: 'Thy kingdom come.' The kingdom is the eradication of the class struggle, of personal and social sin, of unjust and inhuman structures. It is gratuitousness, joy, peace built on justice. It is the radical transformation of the whole universal order, turned into God's dwelling among men. These will be its signs: 'He will wipe away every tear from their eyes, and death shall be no more, neither shall there be mourning nor crying nor pain any more, for the former things have passed away' (Rev. 21:3-4).

6. KNOWING HOW TO PRAY IN THE ELECTRONIC CIVILISATION

Technological progress also tends to de-personalise prayer itself, with worship for the millions, international Eucharistic Congresses, liturgical services on TV. While the churches must fight for their right to free and public religious demonstrations, there is a risk that the ecclesial community will pay a very high political price for this freedom—the preservation of bourgeois neo-Christendom. The bourgeois State is concerned to relay the relationship between the Church and society through its own ideological apparatus. This relaying allows the ruling classes to re-appropriate Christianity, thereby compromising worship itself, since it can become idolatrous through sacralising an unjust order which permits the Church freedoms it denies to its people—the specific case in Argentina, Chile and Guatemala. In social life, Christians have to win space for prayer which can be space for a free demonstration of the voice of the poor. This has been the rôle of the base communities in Latin America. In these, the poor have regained their right to organise themselves, to speak, to develop their critical faculties through comparison between the events narrated in the Bible and the events of their own lives. The Bible is not read like a screeen through which interesting events in the past can be glimpsed. Rather, it is prayed like a glass in which the community *sees and questions* itself.

This contact with the theophanic setting of the poor, relayed through their own ecclesial communities, establishes new conditions and stimuli for personal prayer. It is no longer a case of shunning the city, but of discovering time and space for prayer within it. This does not remove the 'desert' of personal solitude, but allows daily routine to be integrated with intimacy in love, a spiritual parallel with married people in their matrimonial/professional lives.

There is no need to climb mountains or even hills to reach the Father. He pervades our whole lives (Acts 17:28). We only need to open ourselves to his presence and allow the Spirit to pray in us in order to become capable of loving as Jesus loved: open and dedicated to our neighbours (1 John 4:19-21), especially to the neediest among them (James 2:14-15).

Translated by Paul Burns

PART III

The Reception of Vatican II in a Changed Historical Context

Antonio Acerbi

Receiving Vatican II in a Changed Historical Context

IS THE programme put forward by the Council for a renewed presence of the Church in the world still valid? Or, if one prefers to put the question in less radical terms, which aspects of the Council retain their significance for today and for the foreseeable future, and which have lost it with the passage of time? The question is not out of place; it can rightly be asked of any document which is historically determined—which depends, that is, on a precise historical context and sets out not to enunciate propositions that are valid in an abstract way, but rather to relate to a given historical situation—and which at the same time seeks recognition as a normative authority which can transcend the limits of the historical context that produced it. That is to say, one should ask oneself how and to what extent a text formulated 'yesterday', within the context of and dependent on thought patterns and social and religious conditions that are out of date, can have permanent significance also for 'today'.[1]

As far as Vatican II is concerned, the question cannot be avoided, either at the level of fact, since there are those who say that today they are neither in favour of nor against the Council, but simply somewhere else;[2] or at the level of principle, since the Council itself proclaimed its desire to measure up to the men and problem of its time, and in so doing did not conceal, but rather proclaimed its own historicity. No new dogmatic declarations, but a global consideration, pastoral in character, of the entire mission of the Church and the manner in which it is realised in relation to the human situation and of the international society of our (or better, its) time: that was the programme of the Council. Its relationship to the historical moment is therefore not accidental, so that one can rightly ask whether the proposals of the Council are still valid today, in a situation which we experience as profoundly different from that which set the tone of the Council documents.

New ecclesial experiences which have been maturing outside Europe, and mid-European theology's consequent loss of its central position; the arrival in the West of new ethical and cultural models; the crisis of legitimacy in the institutions—these are some of the phenomena that combined to express in different terms certain problems dealt with by the Council: one thinks of the question of the priestly ministry, discussion of which has been profoundly altered by the experience of the 'basic ecclesial communities' in Latin America, or else of the problems of social justice, sexuality or authority in the Church.

1. THE GENERAL CHANGE OF CLIMATE IN WESTERN SOCIETY

I do not mean to undervalue these elements of change, which have called in question the permanent value of certain affirmations of the Council. I maintain, however, that the most decisive factor behind this sense of estrangement from the Council is the general change of climate in western society. I will limit my observations to this, fully aware of the limitation.

I have no difficulty in admitting that for some, above all those who belong to the generation which lived through the Council, and above all if they were theologically aware, the elements of continuity and permanence prevail over those that create division. But in general, and above all for the younger generation, the change in the social climate has in some way distanced the Council, weakening its significance as a global reality, as the bearer of one unbroken meaning through its individual affirmations and of a dynamic force which unifies all the dimensions of the Church's life.

During the 1970s the entire world felt weighed down by international competition for the control of national resources. In those years, both the countries of the West and those of the Socialist bloc adopted a strategy for control of the sources of energy and of the mineral resources of the planet. This strategy was based by and large on the peaceful penetration of those countries that hold such riches, by means of the transfer of technology or favourable commercial agreements, but it could also be expressed in sudden attacks and recourse to forms of military occupation. This strategy, which grew out of the anticipation of scarcity and the apocalyptic forecasts of the MIT and the Club of Rome, formulates the problem of resources as though it were exclusively a matter of nature—the so-called 'limits of development'—and not also of the (good or evil) will of men. It is, therefore, a brutally realistic strategy, conservative and completely lacking in courage. Established in outline at the beginning of the decade, it has emptied the East-West confrontation of all conceptual significance—since socialism and capitalism have proved to be different labels for one and the same drive for power and possession—and sparked off the explosive opposition between North and South, the non-aligned countries and those of the Third World against the countries of the two blocs. In 1973, at the time of the Yom Kippur war, the Arab oil producers, soon followed by others, in full awareness of what they were doing, started the price war, which has upset the financial system and placed many countries, rich and poor, western and otherwise, in a state of crisis. One general consequence of this has been of a psychological nature: people have realised that some certainties are disappearing, among them long-cherished projects for life and development, and that thick clouds are obscuring the prospect both of peace and of greater prosperity for individuals and communities. The 1970s will be remembered, perhaps, as the years of the 'great alarm' for prosperity. A sense of increased precariousness in the political and economic situation of the world became widespread, contributing to a sense of distrust (no organ of power, no institution, no political force seemed adequate to guarantee security), to the spread of violence throughout the fabric of society, and to the decline of sociality. Individuality and one's private world re-established themselves: throughout the West, though in varying degrees, the decade was characterised by a *culture of the Ego* and by a growing appreciation of the values related to personal identity. At the economic level individual initiative came back into its own, although at the same time social energies were mobilised from below (at times in a co-operative and conservative form).

The contrast with the climate of the Sixties could not be greater. That was a world, which, having emerged definitively from the period of post-war reconstruction, emboldened by an economic development and prospects for international peace both of which seemed absurd, appeared to be making its way, albeit with the inevitable difficulties, towards an age of peaceful progress and collaboration; an outpouring of collective energies, originating in the need for political and civil participation, seemed set to flood the institutions like a renewing lymph. Naturally, Christians did not remain untouched by this climate, and in fact the image of a world which was moving ahead, and to which the Church wished to lend its support in terms of both affirmation and of assent, was reflected in the Council.

I repeat that it is the change of climate which forces one to ask, not so much whether this or that declaration of the Council has lasting validity, but whether the Council has a unitary meaning and whether that meaning can and should still be accepted in the Church, notwithstanding and, indeed, on account of the changes that have occurred. This global meaning will also provide the basic hermeneutical criteria for the interpretation of the Council documents.

2. THE FOUNDATION FOR A NEW CRITERION OF LEGITIMACY

I put forward a thesis, which I cannot demonstrate here, but which enables me to respond to the initial question. The Council was not in the first place a machine for churning out documents; rather, it was a great spiritual experience, which involved the Catholic Church and the entire Christian world as well as the bishops and theologians. This spiritual experience became, in theory and practice, the principle of a new legitimacy: certain realities, which were not recognised as legitimate in the Church before the Council, acquired a title of legitimacy and even of right, while the reverse took place for other ideas and practical attitudes. The Council documents are nothing other than the translation into a series of normative texts of that principle of legitimacy. In other words, the spiritual experience of the Council is the locus in which the documents are gathered up and receive their meaning, and it therefore provides the basic hermeneutical criterion. There is a certain parallel to be found in the relationship that exists between the anti-Fascist Resistance in Italy from 1943 to 1945 and the republican constitution of 1948. The new intellectual and political order established by the latter found in the Resistance both the basis for its own justification and its fundamental hermeneutical criterion.[3] The normative text can, therefore, be changed, but only within the framework established by the original event; it is impossible, in fact, to bypass the latter without undermining the legitimacy of the entire intellectual and political order. It is quite clear, in the case of the Council, that there is no question of separating the two aspects: a spiritual event experienced apart from, or worse, in opposition to the texts; or else the texts as interpreted in another context, provided by an experience different from (and even opposed to) that of the Council. The basic event and the documents refer to one another and are mutually illuminating: the meaning of the former is, in fact, translated into the latter and cannot be recovered unless they are taken into account; but the documents, if they are to be understood as they should be, must be passed through the filter of the spiritual experience constituted by the basic event. The task of the interpreter is precisely to pick up this reciprocal dependence and to draw from it the main lines of the new criterion of legitimacy, based on the spiritual experience and sanctioned in the texts. Thus will the work of interpretation be able to bring to light such gradations as are present in the documents. That is to say, it may be that not all the texts reflect the original spiritual experience to the same extent, in which case a certain hierarchy will be recognised among the documents, based on their more or less immediate connection with the basic religious experience, and, by the same token, varying degrees of reformability, or, more precisely, need for reform (on the hypothesis that a given text still reflects a view of things that was superseded by the spiritual experience of the Council).

3. THE SPIRITUAL EXPERIENCE OF THE COUNCIL

As I see it, the experience of the Council expressed in a nutshell, was the reform of the Church for its own mission, under the sign of fidelity to the Word of God. We witnessed in the Council a unique and wonderful event: a vast social grouping, an ancient and highly stabilised institution, embarking with extraordinary sincerity on a programme of research, in order to be more faithful to its own mission. The Catholic community—at every level as well as in its most significant exponents, starting with Pope John XXIII who gave the initial impulse, and then subsequently by Pope Paul VI and the Council fathers who took this impulse up—set out to examine the forms in which its life was expressed, its pastoral experience to date, its traditional social status, and its cultural heritage. The reform of the Church—since that is what we are talking about—was thus not understood or sought as a way of adapting to the times, as a rationalisation based on models borrowed from the secular sciences, or as an accommodation to the demands of the contemporary conscience. Something of all these was, at least in part, at work within the Council enterprise, but it certainly did not provide the tone. The significance of the Council effort is to be found elsewhere. The Church who was questioning herself about her mission and the conditions in which she carried it out, intended to set aside the human securities that were hers as a result of her past, in order to place herself in an attitude of listening and obedience before the Word of God, and to acquire once again the freedom and strength that come from fidelity to the gospel.

The perspectives of ecclesial life which were affirmed during the Council matured historically, certainly, but they were thought out and desired as ways of adhering more immediately and more faithfully to the Word of God, and it is from here that the conciliar innovations received their vitality and unity. Ideas, first put forward by a few theologians and accepted only in certain more or less extensive circles, were taken up as part of an overall project of renewal of the Church and its presence in the world, which gave all these initially scattered ideas their unifying dynamism and their interdependence. What emerged in fact was a sort of *perichoresis* between the ideas, in which the experience of reform through which the Church was passing in fidelity to the gospel, and in the power of the Spirit, was expressed, so that it is impossible to understand one without taking account of the others, or to accept one part of them while rejecting another. The idea of reform itself, as an essential aspect of the Church (*Ecclesia semper reformanda*), received form and content from the idea of the Church as 'mystery'—of its essentially eschatological nature and its relationship to the kingdom, of its historicity and presence within it of sin, of the relative character ('sign and instrument') of its institutional components. The centrality of the Word, the essential rôle of the liturgy, the diffusion of charisms among the people of God, the Catholic unity of the ecclesial body, and recognition of the rôle of the visible aspect of the Church as a sacrament of saving unity were other ideas which made possible a fruitful reconsideration of relationships within the Church and between the different Christian communities. But the principal ideas for a new and evangelical relationship with the world were bathed in the same spiritual atmosphere: such concepts as the positive nature of the world even in the judgment of sin, acceptance of freedom, attentive listening, service, the tension common to both Church and world in relation to the kingdom of God, and, above all, the idea that underlies the whole of *Gaudium et Spes*, namely, that the Church and the world can and should meet one another on the same ground, that of the gospel truth about man and awareness of the emergence of what is new and creative in the course of history (the 'signs of the times').

To conclude, the experience of the Church, reforming herself in the light of the gospel, is the framework within which the Council documents belong and within which, transcending all cultural variations, the unchangeable elements are determined. Had the Council set out to achieve no more than some sort of accommodation to the cultural context of its time, both of the attitudes, which, from opposing sides, the progressive and the conservative, finally manage, in the name of the Council's historicity, to empty it of all significance, would basically be correct. In reality, the principal purpose of the Council precludes its intrinsic dependence on its historical context. Yet it is that same purpose which makes it possible to identify the transient element. The appropriate attitude, it seems to me, is one of acceptance of the conciliar texts in the light of the conciliar experience, the latter being the criterion against which the documents themselves are to be judged, according to whether they show signs of being insufficiently imbued with the conciliar spirit or depend substantially on the cultural and social situation of the moment at which the Council took place. Against this progressive interpretation of the conciliar texts, it is possible to put forward a talmudic interpretation, in which respect for the letter of the text, of any text, fragments the conceptual unit, from which they receive their life and the ability to overcome their limits, and makes it possible to empty these texts of meaning through their insertion into a conceptual and practical context which was not originally theirs. One example of an interpretation that remained faithful to the Council by going beyond the letter of the Council is well known: the liturgical reform, the provisions of which, for example where the vernacular languages were concerned, went beyond the norms laid down in *Sacrosanctum Concilium*, while remaining faithful to the underlying principles of the same constitution. At the present time, it seems that one of the most important aspects of the acceptance of Vatican II is about to be completed, that is, the revision of the Code of Canon Law. To transplant certain affirmations from the context of evangelical renewal in which they originated to the juridical context is one of the most delicate and, to be quite frank, risky of operations. On the ability of the revisers to adapt the Code to the Council will also depend the question whether the latter will continue to be accepted through the institutional channels, or whether it will be ignored by those who maintain that it has lacked the power really to modify the canonical structure and has served, basically, to re-establish the balance between existing elements, or, on the other hand, invoked as a permanent principle of criticism and protest *vis-à-vis* the post-conciliar canonical situation.[4]

4. GOING BEYOND THE COUNCIL TO BE FAITHFUL TO THE COUNCIL

It would be interesting, at this point, to analyse the conciliar documents and to see in detail which formulations are fully in accordance with the fundamental purpose of the Council, which, instead, need to be developed and corrected, and which are irrevocably out of date. However, that is clearly not possible here. Certainly no one would imagine it would be enough to make a list of the ideas and classify them under three heads. Besides, this entire issue of *Concilium* aims, fundamentally, to clarify the problem.

But the diagnosis put forward at the beginning, namely that the present sense of alienation from the Council depends, above all, on the changes in the social climate, prompts reflection on at least one of the documents, namely, *Gaudium et Spes*, which more than any of the others bears the imprint of the historical moment.

In this constitution, an ecclesial 'consensus' was achieved regarding the affirmation that the Church and society must find a point of meeting and reciprocal recognition in the truth about man as revealed in the gospel. To have chosen Christian anthropology as the conceptual 'medium' through which to express the relationship between the Church and the world is to have expressed the terms of that relationship in a radically new way. To establish at their centre the 'mystery' of man, created and redeemed, is to proclaim that at the heart of human history is the 'mystery of Christ', in which man and his activity find their meaning and their fulfilment. The Church, therefore, which has many and essential links with the 'mystery of Christ' but is neither identifiable with it *tout court* nor an adequate expression of it, is not at the centre. These two factors—the centrality of the 'mystery' and the non-conformity between it and the Church—have made it possible to accept without feelings of resentment the fact that the Church is socially of secondary importance and to regard the social process of secularisation as not necessarily being a negation of the rôle and saving presence of Christ. Acceptance of the fact that the Church is socially of secondary importance goes hand in hand with renunciation of the idea of playing a directive rôle in society: 'The twentieth-century Church no longer has to assume responsibility for the direction of civilisation or the promotion of peoples, rather its task is to put the leaven of the gospel into those civilisations and human structures.'[5] The relationship between the Church and the world is not, therefore, enclosed within the framework of 'Catholic and social teaching', if by that is understood an abstract and non-historical systemisation of the principles underlying the social order, aiming at a completeness and a permanence which disregard the conditions and the changes inherent in historical development, and expressing a desire on the part of the Church to guide society in the matter of its adaptation and its life choices. Instead the Church entrusts its presence in the world to the illuminative, critical and constructive power of the gospel message within historical situations. This places the Church, *vis-à-vis* historical movements, in an attitude neither of competition nor of identification, neither of subordination nor of supremacy. What is involved instead is a work of discernment, in which sympathy and critical judgment reveal both the solidarity of Christians with human history as a focus of the redeeming and creative love of God, and their detachment from it, in so far as human godlessness is revealed within it. At this point, it seems to me, the choice of Christian anthropology as the ideal place in which to re-establish the relationship between the Church and the world is so intrinsically bound up with the theological discourse of the Council, on the one hand, and, on the other, with the Church's will to be an evangelical presence in the world, not institutionally and by the use of power but through witness and service, that it would be impossible to reject it without calling in question the fundamental purpose of the Council and, in the last analysis, the legitimacy of the new approach.

It is nevertheless quite true that *Gaudium et Spes* expressed this choice in terms which reflect a limited cultural and historical context. Interest is shown predominantly in those dimensions of the human experience which have been brought to light through personalist reflection, and in those values which constitute perennial points of reference for human life. On the other hand, little or no attention is paid to the impact of the structural data and the positive rather than merely problematical significance of the changes that have been taking place in human history, especially in our own time. The limitation is evident in a particular way in the treatment of certain themes, which are crucial for an evangelical understanding of man: I am thinking, for example, of the theme of peace, and that of poverty.[6]

The political and cultural vicissitudes of the 1970s demonstrated instead that the 'wealth-poverty' dyad is the central point of the international political balance (and closely connected, therefore, with the theme of peace), but the point also at which there emerges a more lively awareness of the new dimensions of human experience, and thus the critical point or an evangelical awareness of man.

In the present-day situation, the Church's effort to practise evangelical poverty is not a feature merely of her internal reform; rather it represents the privileged ground for the meeting between the gospel message and the aspirations of individuals and peoples who find themselves caught between a purely ideological proclamation of freedom and the reality of structures dominated by the strong, in which the weak run the risk of being annihilated or becoming cogs in a machine. In a global society, in which the problem of access to the sources of energy and to raw materials has torn away the last of the conceptual veils which camouflaged the real reasons of governments and economic bodies, and in which the hardening of the conflict brutally excludes all consideration of the arguments of those who have not the strength to make them heard, the choice of evangelical poverty means nothing unless it means awareness of the dependence of situations of poverty on situations of power, and, therefore, involvement of oneself 'together' with the poor in the task they have undertaken in order to become responsible for their own future. Alarm about the threat to their own well-being has blotted out the poor and their rights from the consciousness of the rich. To maintain both the one and the other on the horizon of the Christian conscience is the primary task of the Church, for whom poverty today means above all availability for that essential work of collective justice and universal peace, in which Christians will themselves encounter poverty and the opposition of the powerful.

But acceptance of Vatican II must, in my view, signify also acceptance of the anthropological changes which are emerging from the crisis of the neo-capitalist ideology of 'well-being'. We are more acutely aware today than we were in the past that the neo-capitalist 'well-being' (like the authoritarian planning imposed by 'Diamat') sanctions the prevalence of 'poor' needs over 'rich' needs and leads economically speaking to a levelling out of mankind. Under the banner of the development of production and of well-being, what has been smuggled in, in reality, is the subordination of man to the fetish of consumer goods and the Gross National Product. If the crisis in the world economic system results in the politics of power or, in individuals, the prevalence of personal or corporate egoism, in certain significant if not dominant sectors of the population, especially the young, one is also aware of the growth of the 'need for culture', understood as a search for meaning not as a means of access to power; of the 'need for contemplation', as a non-instrumental form of awareness; of the 'need for communication', as the basis for more authentic forms of socialisation; of the 'need for peace', extended even to the animals and the natural environment. And at the root of all this there is another need, diametrically opposed to the bourgeois and 'orthodox Marxist' tradition: that of a new identity, of a new style of existence, of a new mode of being. Here the need to live in a significant and coherent way merges with the need to be at peace, to express oneself freely, to contemplate and to know. There are truly revolutionary possibilities in all this, and, while being substantially lay in inspiration, it is, of all that has been expressed by the culture of our day, that which comes closest to the spirit of the gospel.

Not a human development unrelated to its material basis—the liberation of man undoubtedly comes through the equal satisfaction of essential needs—but progress through the increase of freedom, personal and collective, to express those values by which the individual and the community wish to live, through the voluntary renunciation of domination, possession, success and social recognition: this is a 'sign of the times', at the heart of which the Church is called to proclaim the message of God, which is supreme freedom and gratuitousness, and the infinite gift made to man in order that the latter might discover himself as freedom, gratuitousness and gift of self.

Acceptance of the Council, for *Gaudium et Spes* as for the rest, is not, therefore, a work of mechanical transposition. It is a work of courage and imagination, of that imagination which *Octogesima Adveniens* requires of Christians, but which is lacking today in those parts of the world which count for something and have a say in things. Will the Church be able to move against the current? To predict that it will mean not only to give oneself a goal worthy of effort, but also to place one's trust in the Spirit, who still sustains her, today as during the years of the Council.

Translated by Sarah Fawcett

Notes

1. This questioning of the permanent validity of Vatican II is not unique. It is, for example, at the centre of Karl Rahner's paper 'Il significato permanente del Vaticano II *Il Regno doc.* 3 (1980) 73-77. On the general problem of acceptance of the Council, see Yves Congar 'Reception as an Ecclesiological Reality' *Concilium* 7 (1972) 43.

2. In this sense, see J.-P. Jossua 'Il metodo teologico conciliare e la teologia oggi' (paper read at the conference 'Ricezione del concilio nella vita della chiesa e della società', Bologna, 3-7 December 1975) *Il Regno doc.* 5 (1976) 132-133. On the problem in general, see *Le Déplacement de la théologie* (Actes du colloque méthodologique de février 1976), edited by the Institut Catholique de Paris, Paris 1977.

3. On the significance of the anti-Fascist Resistance for the Italian Constitution of 1948, see *The Rebirth of Italy 1943-1950* ed. J. Stuart Woolf (London 1972), especially the essay of E. Gheli; *Costituente et lotta politica* ed. R. Ruffilli (Florence 1978); *Cultura politica e partiti nell'età della Constituente* ed. R. Ruffilli, two volumes (Bologna 1979).

4. On the connection between the Council documents and the final draft of the Lex Ecclesiae Fundamentalis, see A. Abelli 'Ein Grungesetz der Restauration? Zum Entwurf einer "Lex Fundamentalis" der Kirche' *Herder Korrespondenz* 33 (1979) 1, 36-43.

5. M. D. Chenu 'Consecratio mundi' *Nouvelle Revue Théologique* (1964) 615.

6. For a detailed analysis of *Gaudium et Spes* and of its value, see A. Acerbi *La Chiesa nel tempo. Sguardi sui progetti di relazion tra Chiesa a società civile negli ultimi centi anni* (Milan 1979) pp. 182-232.

BULLETINS

Gabriel Marc

Statistical Data, Projections and Interpretations Relating to the Numerical Composition of the Catholic Church

DECOLONISATION marks the end of an age of mission. The proclamation of the gospel for the future demands new methods and attitudes.

A look at a map of religions shows that religions are distributed in precise geographical areas, evidence of the strength of historical links between cultures, peoples and religions. While religious minorities exist in many countries, those in which religious pluralism really exists are few. There are some in the white world, but most are in Africa, where traditional animism is on the retreat, apparently before the missionary pressure of Islam and, secondarily, of the Christian religions. It is almost inevitable that the missionary expansion of one religion should take place in the geographical region of another or as the result of unequal birth rates.

In fact, however, even in their areas of expansion, the great religions are yielding to the combined blows of technical civilisation, urbanisation, mobility and the mass media. Gaps are appearing in all the continents, forming areas open to the preaching of religion.

This raises the question whether Catholicism (and Christianity more generally) is showing itself capable of success in this new age of mission when it has to face disaffection even in its traditional area of implantation.

A reply obviously requires more than a few pages. This article will therefore be limited to the basic data obtainable from a comparison of the Church's Statistical Directory, the world report of the United Bible Societies, the yearbooks of the United Nations and the World Bank. It will also be limited to three aspects. These will be sufficient to guide a consideration of mission.

1. THE 'NATURAL MOVEMENT' OF THE CATHOLIC POPULATION

1.1 At the beginning of 1978 the Catholic Church claimed almost 750 million baptised, or 18 per cent of the world population. The total for Christians of all denominations is nearly 1,200 million, or almost 29 per cent of the world population.

There are two main Catholic areas, containing 90 per cent of Catholics: Europe and North America (the 'western world') with 44 per cent, and Latin America and the Philippines with 46 per cent. The remainder is distributed in the proportions of 2 per cent in Asia, 7 per cent in Africa and 1 per cent in Oceania.

Perhaps the reality revealed by these figures of implantation is a commonplace to informed observers, but it has not yet penetrated western attitudes. *There are more Catholics in Latin America than in Europe. There are more Catholics outside the western world than inside it. The only major continental region in which Catholicism is dominant is Latin America.* On the other hand, the Church's base is in Europe. Europe is still the source of the rules of all kind which are imposed on the universe. Europe still provides the majority of the Church's administrators. This is a distortion which, if not corrected, could eventually become paralysing and even create conflict.

1.2 The Catholic Church is associated with high birth rates. However, if Catholics are divided according to the average birth rates of the countries in which they live and the result compared with the same division of the world's population, we find notable divergences. 44 per cent of Catholics (68 per cent of Protestants), but only 27 per cent of the human race, live in countries with very low birth rates, less than 20 per 1,000. On the other hand, 39 per cent of Catholics (27 per cent of Protestants) and 31 per cent of the human race live in countries with high birth rates, rates of over 35 per 1,000. Once again we find a contrast within Catholicism between a tired western world and a vigorous African and Latin American world. This has two consequences:

> Almost half of all Catholics live in countries where young people under 16 form no more than 25 per cent and, less frequently, 30 per cent of the population, while the other half live in countries where such young people form more than 40 per cent. The population in the countries which set the tone in the Church is so old that it inevitably creates a mentality predominantly concerned with the past, traditionalist and conservative. This is a definite handicap in a world in which young people form 36 per cent of the population.

> Everything else being equal, the mass of non-western Catholics will become numerically more and more important in the Church. If they remain in a position of inferiority, with no chance to express their cultures in the production of Church rules, there is reason to fear dissatisfaction or even splits. The first signs are already visible.

1.3 This demographic information can be used to project the Catholic population, for example, in the year 2000. However, there is an important corrective to be kept in mind. If we compare, for all the countries of the world, the rate of baptisms in the Catholic population and the birth rate in the population as a whole, we find that the former is almost everywhere lower than the latter. The only exceptions are the vigorous little churches of Asia, Central Africa and Eastern Africa, Nigeria and finally North America, Australia and New Zealand, where Catholic immigrants are numerous. This is a sign that the missionary vigour and the appeal of Catholicism are in decline.

By applying this corrective, we can produce a figure of 950 million, or 15 per cent of the world population, for the total of Catholics in the year 2000. Asia (not including the Philippines) will by then contain 60 per cent of the human race and only 4 per cent of Catholics. This shows clearly where mission is most urgent.

This reduction in the percentage of Catholcis in the world population does not take into account the number of 'floating' believers now found in many countries. For want of firm figures this cannot be quantified everywhere, but surveys show that, particularly in Europe, religious practice is becoming a minority phenomenon, vague religious affiliation without practice is becoming widespread and ending in paganism. In a country like France respondents claiming 'no religion' are, on average, as numerous as regular worshippers and much more numerous among young adults between 20 and 35.

The general impression left by a rapid survey of the figures is of a sort of arthritis. Western Catholicism remains normative, obsessed with the past, and cannot bring itself to give room to the vigour of the cuttings it has planted in other soils. The paradox is that the people with the faith and the imagination have no voice while those whose voices are heard shut themselves up in ghettos to avoid doubt and have no ideas. There seems little hope of being able to get to grips with mission in the world as it is without firm action to solve this paradox.

2. PARALYSING STRUCTURES

The generally recognised strength of the Catholic Church is its organisation. This is also its weakness because its rigidity, size, and complexity have much to do with the arthritic state we have noted. The Church is showing itself insufficiently supple to adapt to the cultural diversity of nations and the critical developments in human history through which we are passing, and shall perhaps be passing for several decades.

The organisational structure is marked by two features which go together, a hierarchical geographical pattern and another hierarchical pattern in relations between clergy and the rest of the baptised.

2.1 A detailed study based on the *Annuario Pontificio* shows that *the average size of a diocese is very large* in relation both to the general population and the number of believers.

There are of course considerable differences between one continent and another. In Oceania, Africa and Asia, on the whole countries evangelised quite recently, dioceses contain on average a number of Catholics between 65,000 and 130,000 which is in itself a lot, and populations of more than a million, which is clearly excessive. But what are we to think of the average size in Europe and Latin America of over 400,000 Catholics. How can the leaders of these dioceses be really close to their people and have direct knowledge of their needs?

These were only continental averages. There are 131 dioceses in the world with between one and seven million Catholics. The population of the largest diocese, Mexico, would make it 67th among the member countries of the UN if it were a nation! 36 per cent of Catholics live in such giant dioceses in Europe, Latin America and the Philippines.

In Europe and North America 21 dioceses have staffs of priests, men and women religious numbering over 7,500. The administration of such organisations inevitably absorbs the bulk of available energy and the Catholic people practically disappears from the view of its pastors, who still speak confidently in their name in the central forums of the Church's government.

The main consequence of such vast size is *unsuitability for evangelisation in the modern city*. The city is a new and attractive sociological phenomenon. It already contains a quarter of the inhabitants of the earth, and still represents a challenge for governments, local authorities and religions. An unsuitable religious structure will not fit easily into it, all the more when those responsible for its management are crushed beneath the weight of their organisations. Dioceses would have to be increased in number by ten or twenty to produce an effective machine for work in the city.

2.2 The second tier of parishes and their clergy might seem a suitable substitute where dioceses become too large. It is true that it has fulfilled this function of immediate contact with the people for a long time, and continues to do so where the network of ecclesial communities coincides with that of human communities. This, however, is ceasing to be the case in an increasing number of circumstances, notably in the mobile

G

society of the modern city. Territoriality gives the Church a certain visibility, but corresponds to only one of the many types of sociological grouping of citizens. By sticking to it we are in danger of failing to reach many people.

The problem also exists, however, increasingly often in the less populated rural areas, where the population is scattered and the number of priests tiny. This situation, frequent outside Europe in the poor countries, creates a distance between the local basic community and the distant parish. These basic communities, which take responsibility for their own lives as best they can, are multiplying outside Europe and it is no secret that the Church's government is reluctant to recognise them and to encourage the ministries to which they give rise.

The different situation in Europe and North America is due to the fact that hitherto there have been no staffing problems. In Europe there is one priest for 1,100 Catholics, and one for 850 in North America. These figures soar to 2,250 in Asia, 3,300 in Africa and more than 6,000 in Latin America. The problems faced by the latter groups have made little impact on the former, who were convinced that this was a transitory stage in the life of the young churches.

The situation is exactly the opposite. The young churches of Asia and Africa are experiencing an increase of vocations. Latin America, on the other hand, cannot provide itself with sufficient priests to meet the needs of its Christian community. Above all, the rate of replacement of the clergy in Europe is simply disastrous, with one or two exceptions. The average age of the clergy is the highest in the world. For every two priests who die only one is ordained. This means that the relationship between priests and people will drift towards what it is in the rest of the world. This does not create a situation particularly favourable to missionary development, unless there is a decision to turn lay people from passive recipients of sacraments to agents of evangelisation. Vatican II offers a whole range of such possibilities, but it is necessary that fear of the consequences on the status of priests and laity should not produce a paralysis of the will.

3. THE MAJOR CONTRADICTION

The main handicap to a renewal of mission at the moment is the ambiguity of the proclamation of the gospel. This is a criticism of Christianity as a whole since at this level all Christians, and not just Catholics, are guilty of counter-testimony to the gospel before the world. The North-South divide runs through Christianity in a way which seriously affects its credibility.

To show this we need only classify Christians according to the *per capita* GDP of the countries in which they live.

41 per cent of Catholics (49 per cent of Christians) live in countries in which the *per capita* GDP in 1977 was more than 3,000 dollars, whereas only a quarter of the world's population, exactly 25 per cent, live in these countries.

In contrast, only 15 per cent of Christians and Catholics live in countries where the *per capita* GDP is below 500 dollars and where 58 per cent of the human race live. Only 5 per cent of Christians belong to the poorest quarter of the world's population!

A mere glance at these crude figures is enough to show anyone that a gospel allegedly proclaimed first to the poor, God's favourites, is in the hands of the rich.

Of course these particular rich are not short of arguments to justify this paradox. They say, for example, that the Christian vision of the world contains the seed of economic growth. This is not an evangelical argument for the poor masses who know from experience how much of their substance has been taken from them by the growth of the rich.

It will be seen that the Christian countries of Latin America bulk large in the middle areas, of a *per capita* GDP between 500 and 3.000 dollars. In appearance, therefore, these are not poor countries. On the other hand it is important not to forget that in these countries income inequalities are very large and still growing. National averages thus conceal ultra-rich minorities living off ultra-poor masses, and both call themselves Christians. This situation contributes to Christianity's absence of credibility.

In this situation of not only economic but also military paradox—because the rich Christian countries are also the ones who pay vast sums to provide themselves with the most horrifying weapons—world evangelisation is impossible. Who could believe in the veracity of the beatitudes when those who proclaim them as their faith impose unequal terms of trade, deny justice within the international community, maintain racial discrimination, practise torture and violate the basic rights of the weakest members of the human race.

Too firmly divided into countries and groups living in contradiction with the gospel they profess, trapped in clumsy structures ill-suited to modern society, deaf to the appeals and ideas of the poor, Catholicism is badly placed for the new age of mission.

It is clear that the future of mission depends, in contrast, on the Church's readiness to welcome the Christianity of the poor, notably the masses of Latin America, and on firm, large-scale action in support of justice, solidarity, peace and respect for human rights.

Translated by Francis McDonagh

Severino Dianich

The Current State of Ecclesiology

THIS ARTICLE aims at taking stock of current ecclesiology, to which two recent congresses have drawn attention. At Bologna in April 1980 about forty theologians, canonists, sociologists and historians, chiefly European and Catholic but also involving non-Catholic experts and persons from other parts of the world, examined in particular the development of the internal structures of the Catholic Church since the Council.[1] At the end of February there was held at São Paulo in Brazil the IVth Congress of the Ecumenical Association of Third World Theology, when representatives from forty-two countries debated the ecclesiology of mass Christian communities.[2] The first meeting, although having the greatest possible awareness of the relation to the world, concentrated on the Church's structures in its universal components and in the make-up of local churches. The second meeting, in its final document, seems almost to want to leave aside these problems to consider the mission of the Church at its local, popular level. This divergence is already an interesting sign of two different ways of doing ecclesiology: the first characteristic of the older theological tradition, the second belonging more to the theology of the younger churches and those of Latin-America.

1. AFTER THE COUNCIL: SEARCHING FOR A NEW EQUILIBRIUM

The immediate post-conciliar period does not yield a unified hermeneutical direction in ecclesiology. Rather it receives, correctly and gladly, the conciliar thrust towards plenitude, totality and multiplicity of interpretative routes. The first task of the theologians is aimed at substantive research, in biblical and patristic sources, on the images and formulations that the Council copiously used when talking of the Church. It would appear that the dominant interest was in the notion of sacrament and the possibility of defining the Church as sacrament, even if complicated problems make this difficult. Further on we shall see this in detail. Only at a later time does it become possible to study more deeply the ecclesiology of the Council, and then its limits, conditioning factors and contradictions emerge. It emerges, for example, that the difficulty in gaining momentum for collegiality and for a more harmonious development in the relationship of the universal to particular churches, is not only to be attributed to the wishes of certain people but also to the operation in the Council of two differing ecclesiological perspectives, one based on community, the other on society, not dovetailed perfectly.[3] The communitarian perspective, indeed adopted by the Council, should have produced, moreover, a definite restructuring of the Church's relation to the hierarchic ministry. Fr Congar, for his part, accepts the need to rewrite several pages of his famous *Jalons pour une théologie du laicat*, so as to comprehend ministry as an articulation of the community rather than as a structure mediating between God and the community.[4] This problem helped to make increasingly disquieting the stormy debate over the ecclesial status of the priest.[5] With this background, one asks today if we can talk of a community's 'right' to have a priest, where it is the community as subject-church that focuses on itself the question, and it is not the hierarchical institution that poses itself the question of the community's duties towards it.[6] We are not without instances of the argument being pushed further, arriving at the hypothesis of a community capable of celebrating the Eucharist, albeit in exceptional cases, even without a duly ordained minister.[7]

The shift of interest towards the Church as community also entails, beyond the need for new internal arrangements, a different relationship with the world. In fact it is not always clear if in the above debates what matters most is to redefine the Church from within or to settle its relationship with the world. The collapse of the concept of the *societas perfecta* empties the vast space formerly occupied by the Church in society. It thus comes about that in examining the conciliar documents we talk about *Lumen Gentium* and look at *Gaudium et Spes*, but end up by discovering that the latter document, the most criticised of them all, both from the left and the right, despite its far from slight anachronisms[8] is the text with the most consequences and the richest in effects in the development of ecclesiological thought.

What has emerged so far from our description already explains the difficulty of attempting to elaborate a speculative synthesis of the subject.[9] As a consequence, nothing analogous to the treatise *De ecclesia* in preconciliar theology has emerged from the ecclesiological reflection of these years. Even the most serious attempts to form a synthesis often consist simply in choosing a category or an image with which to traverse ecclesiological topics from a particular point of view, interpreting in a lively manner what one meets and omitting what falls outside the programmed route. In this lies the attraction of returning into the thick forest of patristic images therein to remeditate the Church anew. From this point of view the no longer recent works of De Lubac, Von Balthasar, Casel, Hugo Rahner, etc., have still a very important function to play.[10]

2. THE ECCLESIOLOGY OF THE SACRAMENT

With ecclesiology in this state, one systematic approach is, however, being given particular attention, and it is that of the sacramental interpretation of the Church.[11] The best known work is Semmelroth's, published in 1954, but which significantly was only translated into Italian and French in the period of the Council's sessions.[12] Semmelroth does not claim great speculative ambitions for himself, and his ecclesiology seems to find in the idea of sacrament more an instrument capable of illustrating many aspects of the Church than a true and proper hermeneutical and critical principle.[13] Karl Rahner, on the other hand, in following this path, benefits from the advantages that come to him from having described it against the ground of his ontology, where all being and each being is symbolic, in that it is and it expresses itself and in expressing itself acquires self-realisation.[14] Accordingly he considers all history as a manifesting and realising of salvation, that is of the self-communication of God to man. Only that whilst the other historical signs are ambiguous categories, arising from the ambiguity of the yes and the no uttered by man to God who communicates himself, the history of Jesus is achieved realisation, victorious in his resurrection, of the self-communication of God to man, and 'the Church, as permanent presence of Jesus Christ in time and space in the shape of the fruit of salvation that can no longer be destroyed' is its fundamental sacrament. The Church is 'not the sign of a mere question from God put to his creature, of which one would not know the effective reply from the world, but rather the sign of a question which, seen in the totality of mankind's history, is active of itself and carries with it its own positive answer'.[15] In this basic context of the Church-as-sacrament the 'seven sacraments' have their life as the actions in which the real symbol of the Church expresses and actualises itself.

In Schillebeeckx[16] the very same approach unfolds on the basis of an elaborate anthropology rather than in terms of an exclusively ontological foundation. The visible and invisible being of man leads to the encounter with God taking place along the lines of sacramentality, so that visible events in history become signs and instruments of inner events, in which God encounters man and saves him. The Christ-event is the primordial sacrament, and the historical entity in which salvation now comes about is the Church, whose focal points are the 'seven sacraments'. This sacramental being of the Church is situated in the totality of all the religious history of mankind, where God is always and by every means sought in and through visible signs and objects: Christian sacramental rites, in fact, are rooted in the primordial symbolic fabric making up the deep layer of the psyche.[17]

This kind of ecclesiology has enjoyed a great success and spread very widely; it is far richer and more complex than appears from these few lines, which are meant to recall its main points rather than to explain it to those who are unaware of it. This ecclesiology aims less, it seems, at meeting the need to understand the Church in itself and more at the necessity of understanding the Church's relation to the world, and to pilot its activity towards the new shores of dialogue and evangelisation. In fact the sacramental perspective overcomes the gap between rites and existence, between the saving meaning of history and the saving mission of the Church. In this lies the key to its success, but here are also revealed some of its weaknesses, exposing it to a multiple critique, coming from various fronts. The sacramental conception of the Church seems to some to enclose it within boundaries that remain introverted and cultic,[18] whilst to others it so opens it to a world which is itself by now experienced to such a high degree as sacramental that the Church drowns in it, totally losing its identity.[19] This ecclesiology, by providing an interpretative formula, that of sacrament, allows one to 'say', to make explicit, to observe the mystery of the Church but does not offer criteria by which to evaluate, judge, discern. The crucial point remains in the end unresolved. Where is the 'divine', or as Rahner would say 'the victorious', in a Church so human and so often defeated? If the *opus operatum* that has taken place in Christ has one of its infallible presences in the *opus operatum* of the seven sacraments, when and how does it transfer its divine efficacy to the *opus operantis ecclesiae*? And the question affects the notion of mission, in which one ought to be able to recognise the divine and the human, so as to be capable of distinguishing where the *oboedientia fidei* is required and where the need to make a judgment and in such a way that the human dimension is not left so shorn of anything concrete and substantial as to be totally adrift in the 'transcendental' and to become even in the Church a kind of anonymous Christianity.[20] This is so much the case that when H. Küng comes to examine the crucial problem of the nature of the Church in the historical character of its forms, he cannot rely on the *theologumenon* of the sacrament, but builds his argument around the themes of the kingdom and of the life-giving Spirit in the dialectic of the 'already and not yet'.[21]

3. THE ECCLESIOLOGY OF MISSION

Thus somewhat inevitably the problem of working out a set of criteria to supply the instruments by which to assess the quality or the degree, the fallibility or the infallibility of sacraments moved to the centre of debate at the VIIth Congress of the Italian Theological Association.[22] There the problem of the criteria for mission did not at all seem to belong properly to a particular heading of ecclesiology, but rather to be at the centre of the whole of ecclesiology. If the notion of mission depends on the conception one has of the Church, it is also true that the conception of the Church depends on the way one understands its mission. The maxim '*agere sequitur esse*' no longer finds in the realm of ecclesiology calm and accepted applications if the Church has to be thought of as in tension towards the kingdom and, therefore, in essential connection with the world and its history. The changing world and the representations, differing from age to age, by which one envisages the future of the kingdom influence greatly the Church's awareness of its mission and thus of its very being. The sweep of the theology of secularisation and then of political theology directs ecclesiology to the unfamiliar territory of a search for the nature of the Church which does not precede but follows on, and is determined by, the questions the world poses the Church. In any case, even in terms of a sacramental perspective, L. Boff had explicitly declared that the idea of a sacrament is not part of a synthesis within the Church but is directed to legitimating it in front of the world, because today the Church's self-awareness is essentially determined by having its origin from God and its existence for the world. In relation to the world the Church has its own specific identity, but it is also within the world a function of that world which must be thought of, in Augustinian terms, as '*gravidus Christo*'.[23]

This widespread desire to overcome ecclesiocentrism becomes at times so imbued with an activist mentality, characteristic of our times, as to place the Church at the service of the world in such a way that its shape and form are completely derived from the requests for salvation that historical man makes, not conditioning its reply in terms of anything other than the criterion of the historical efficiency of its saving mission. Most times, however, one is well aware of the ideological component in the make-up of the activist appeal to the Church and the absolute need to unmask it. Indeed, no one perhaps as much as the Church in the name of the risen crucified one, can take part in every historical movement in reply to the historical needs of man. The Church inserts itself in those historical movements with a specific critical force that allows it to go further in the search really to create a '*homo novus*'. According to some, this critical function in relation to praxis and its hidden ideologies would even be a specific mark of the Church's mission in the world.[24]

This set of problems in the churches of the Third World and of Latin America takes on its own characteristics. Here the experience of a Church coming to birth in countries recently evangelised, and the analogous experience of a Church being reborn in the grass-root communities of Latin America, introduce into theological reflection the needs of an ecclesiogenesis that is coming to terms with the problems of 'inculturation' in Africa and Asia and those of the integration of a people oppressed and struggling for its liberation in Latin American countries.[25] It can happen that in the western world that has become secularised, strongly ideological and post-Christian in character, ecclesiology is pushed into looking for the legitimation of the Church above all in the historical efficiency of its mission, characterised almost by a loss of identity and the progressive spread of self-secularisation. On the other hand, the novel experience of ecclesiogenesis makes the Church more keenly aware of being part of that *actio Dei* which, alone, saves the world. It does not at all appear that the effort of the Churches of Africa and Asia to have their own cultural expression, or the struggle for liberation of the oppressed people of Latin America, must in any way happen at the cost of a loss of identity by the Church or its loss of belief in the God who saves us in Christ. In these terms a characteristic work would seem to me to be that of a Moltmann who is so much in contact with the theology of liberation and at the same time constructs an ecclesiology rigorously based on the Trinitarian missions.

Besides, no ecclesiology more than that of the post-Tridentine period so lacked any Trinitarian perspective and was so engaged in a secular fashion in integrating the Church into society, proclaiming it the 'perfect society', and designing it as the perfect form of a society that should have found in the Church its ultimate consecration to lead from the penultimate to the ultimate goal. In that world-view the opposition of gospel to world was hid in individual ascesis or became politicised in the clash between secular and ecclesiastical power, without being able to be the soul of a fruitful dialectic between the Church and society thereby saving both the Church's identity and its active presence in society. There are many reasons for that situation coming about, but not last is the absence of a Trinitarian background in the conception of the Church and its mission. The Church's exclusively Christological derivation seemed in a certain sense to guarantee its divinity not through the messianic originality of the Son, led by the Spirit towards death and resurrection, but rather by a kind of ontological and juridical status in terms of which no society could have regarded itself as fully legitimate except in respect of the divine prerogative of the Church. The present recovery of the Church's pneumatological dimension not only enriches and actively shapes its internal structure[26] but allows the Church to root itself in the memory of the Christ-event and his founding activity, without losing the dynamism of the Spirit which projects it towards the future in search for the 'truth in its entirety'. And from Christ the Church not only draws a kind of divinisation of its structures but also all its rich relationship with men and with the Father, truly participating in humanity and divinity, and being the bearer in humanity of the transcendence of the divine and in divinity of the obedience of the human. The reality of the incarnation and the reality of the distinction between Father and Son give to the saving mission a dialectic that only a Trinitarian vision of God makes possible and that the Church relives in its mission. Thus the Church interprets itself and its mission by the dialectical pattern of the mission of the Son and of the Spirit, of the issuing from the Father and the return to him by way of the cross and resurrection, of the memory of the incarnation and of the tension towards 'the truth in its totality'. Only from the Trinitarian history of God in the world and with the world can the Church be brought to awareness of its being crucified to the world together with the poor and the defeated of the earth, and of being at the same time the power of the resurrection and the leaven of the world's future. A Trinitarian perspective seems, then, to be the most interesting one for ecclesiology, capable of giving fruitful developments in the understanding of the Church's mission in history, as well as of the Church's very nature.[27]

It goes without saying that this rapid survey of the most important events in the field of ecclesiology in these last years ought to be expanded to take account of the lively discussions on the theme of primacy and collegiality, of infallibility, of councils and their reception, of the many disputed points of ecumenism, of the place of the sacraments in the Church, of the ordained ministry, etc. These isolated themes, however, acquire their greatest importance above all when seen in relation to the fundamental conceptions of the Church, from which any single ideas derive or to which they imperceptibly lead. Only the theme of mission, at one time considered a particular heading, seems to have shown itself not as one among several topics of ecclesiology but rather as *the* area in which to pose the fundamental question concerning the nature of the Church.[28]

Translated by Robert Ombres

Notes

1. See the concluding paper by J. M. R. Tillard published in *Il Regno—Documenti* 25, n. 420 pp. 273-277.

2. See the last document in *Il Regno—Documenti* 25, n. 418 pp. 223-229.

3. A. Acerbi *Due ecclesiologie. Ecclesiologia giuridica ed ecclesiologia di comunione nella 'Lumen Gentium'* (Bologna 1975).

4. Y. Congar *Ministère et communion ecclésiale* (Paris 1971).

5. S. Dianich *Il prete: a che serve? Saggio di teologia del ministero ordinato* (Rome 1978) including ample assessments of recent literature.

6. *Concilium* 133 (1980) 'The Right of the Community to a Priest'.

7. H. Küng *Die Kirche* (Freiburg 1967) pp. 520-522 (ET *The Church* London 1967 pp. 442f); L. Boff *Ecclesiogenesi* (Rome 1978) pp. 101-114.

8. J.-P. Jossua 'Il metodo teologico conciliare e la teologia oggi' *Il Regno—Documenti* 21, n. 5 pp. 132-133.

9. A recent collection of the most relevant items produced in this area can be found in B. Mondin *Le nuove ecclesiologie* (Rome 1980).

10. See the ample bibliography by J. Frisque 'L'ecclesiologia nel XX secolo' *Bilanz der Theologie im 20. Jahrhundert* ed. R. Vander Gucht and H. Vorgrimler (Freiburg Br. 1970) III 192-243.

11. M. Bernards 'Zur Lehre von der Kirche als Sakrament' *Münchener Theologische Zeitschrift* 20 (1969) 29-54.

12. O. Semmelroth *Die Kirche als Ursakrament* (Frankfurt a.M. 1953).

13. See the review by Y. Congar in *Revue des Sciences Philosophiques et Théologiques* 37 (1953).

14. The thought of K. Rahner, scattered in several works, is given in summary form in *Grundkurs des Glaubens* (Freiburg i. Br. 1976; ET *Foundations of Christian Faith* London 1978).

15. *Ibid.* p. 523.

16. E. Schillebeeckx *Christus, Sacrament van de Godsonmoeting* (Bilthoven 1960; ET *Christ the Sacrament* London 1963); *La Mission de l'Eglise* (Brussels 1969).

17. L. Bouyer *Le Rite et l'Homme* (Paris 1962; ET *Rite and Man* London 1963).

18. L. Rütti *Zur Theologie der Mission* (München 1972) pp. 50-62.

19. H. U. Von Balthasar *Cordula oder der Ernstfall* (Einsiedeln 1966).

20. A dense critique of the idea of the Church as *Ursakrament* is by G. Colombo 'Dove va la teologia sacramentaria?' in *La Scuola Cattolica* 102 (1974) pp. 673-717.

21. H. Küng *The Church* cited in note 7.

22. *Coscienza e missione di Chiesa* (under the auspices of ATI) (Assisi 1977).

23. L. Boff *Die Kirche als Sakrament im Horizontder Welterfahrung* (Paderborn 1972).

24. See N. Greinacher 'Das Theorie-Praxis Problem in der Praktischen Theologie' ed. F. Klostermann and R. Zerfass *Praktische Theologie Heute* (Munich 1974) pp. 103-118.

25. W. Bühlmann *Es Kommt die Dritte Kirche* (Rome 1974); L. Boff *Ecclesiogenesi*, cited in note 23. See also G. Gutierrez's contribution at the Bologna Congress mentioned above (forthcoming).

26. H. Mühlen *Una Mystica Persona* (Paderborn 1964); G. Hasenhüttl *Charisma. Ordnungsprinzip der Kirche* (Freiburg Br. 1969); N. Afanassief *L'Eglise du Saint Esprit* (Paris 1975).

27. J. Moltmann *Die Kirche in der Kraft des Geistes* (Munich 1975; ET *The Church in the Power of the Spirit* London 1977); H. U. Von Balthasar *Herrlichkeit* III/3 *Neuer Bund* (Einsiedeln 1969; ET in preparation); W. Kasper and G. Sauter *Kirche Ort des Geistes* (Frieburg Br. 1976).

28. S. Dianich 'La Missione della Chisa nella Teologia Recente' in *Coscienza e Missione di Chiesa*, cited in note 22, 137-206; 427-440.

Contributors

ANTONIO ACERBI was born at Lodi (Milan) in 1935 and ordained to the priesthood in 1964. He was awarded a degree in jurisprudence at the Catholic University of Milan in 1958, and another in theology in the Theology Faculty of the same in 1972. He specialises in the history of the Church and the history of theology. His principal publications are: 'Due ecclesiologie. Ecclesiologia giuridica ed ecclesiologia di communione' in *Lumen Gentium* (Bologna 1975); *Il diritto nella Chiesa. Tensioni e sviluppi nella storia* (Brescia 1977); *La Chiesa nel tempo. Sguardi sui progetti di relazioni tra Chiesa e Società negli ultini cento anni* (Milan 1979).

D. S. AMALORPAVADASS was born in India in 1932 and ordained priest of Pondicherry Archdiocese in 1959. He did his specialisation at Institut Catholique de Paris and took a doctorate in systematic theology and Master's degree in pastoral catechetics. The two dissertations which he wrote here were subsequently published: *Destinee de L'Eglise dans L'Inde d'aujourd'hui* (Paris 1966); *L'Inde a la recontre du Seigneur* (Paris 1964). Since February 1967 he has been founder-Director of the National Biblical, Catechitical and Liturgical Centre of India, Bangalore (NBCLC) and has been appointed by the Catholic Bishops' Conference of India (CBCI) as Secretary of three National Episcopal Commissions for Liturgy, Catechetics and for the Bible. He is a consultant of a few dicasteries of the Holy See. He was a Special Secretary of the Synod of Bishops in Rome in 1974, a member of Vatican delegation to the V Assembly of WCC, 1975, and World Conference on Mission, Melbourne 1980, and has been a member of the Joint Working Group (JWG) between RCC and WCC since 1976. He is founder-editor of the two monthly reviews: 'Thozhan' from 1959-1965 and 'Word and Worship' from 1967 till now. He has published numerous articles in Indian and foreign reviews, and has published or edited many other books of catechetical, liturgical, biblical and ecumenical nature.

FREI BETTO (Carlos Libanio Christo) was born in Brazil in 1944, first imprisoned by the military régime there in 1964 and joined the Dominicans in 1965, making his solemn profession as a lay brother in 1969. Imprisoned again for harbouring political refugees from 1969-73, he then worked with the base communities in the archdiocese of Vitoria. Since 1979 he has been responsible for pastoral work in São Bernardo do Campo, São Paulo. A member of the International Association of Third World Theologians, his works include *Cartas da Prisão* (1975), and *Puebla para o Povo* (1979). His 'Letters from Prison' has been translated into Italian, French, English, Dutch, Spanish and Swedish.

KARI ELISABETH BØRRESEN was born in Oslo, Norway, in 1932. She studied the history of ideas in Oslo, has also studied in Paris and Rome, and is the author of

Subordination and Equivalence. The nature and role of women in Augustine and Thomas Aquinas (Washington 1981: ET of Oslo-Paris 1968). She is at present attached to the Norwegian Scientific Research Council and is on the Committee of the International Association for Patristic Studies. In 1977-79 she was visiting professor in theology in the Gregorian University, Rome, and in 1981 is visiting professor in the Protestant Theology Faculty of Geneva University.

MARIE-DOMINIQUE CHENU, O.P., a Dominican, is a former rector of the Faculties of Saulchoir (Paris), and a former professor in the Faculty of Theology in Paris. His more recent publications include: *L'Evangile dans le temps* (Paris 1964), *Peuple de Dieu dans le monde* (Paris 1966), and *La Doctrine sociale de l'Eglise comme idéologie* (Brescia 1977, Paris 1979). These represent the application to our time of the method he had used for the middle ages, namely, the study of theology in its sociological setting.

SEVERINO DIANICH was born in Fiume (Rijeka) in 1934. He graduated from the Gregorian University, was ordained priest in 1958 and has for quite some time been parish priest of a small community in the diocese of Pisa. He concentrates on ecclesiology, particularly on aspects of the ordained ministry. His chief publications in this area are: *La Chiesa Ministero di Comunione* (Torino 1979); the entry 'Ecclesiologia' in *Dizionario Teologico Interdisciplinare* (Torino 1977) III, 17-31; *Il Prete: A Che Serve? Saggio di Teologia del Ministero Ordinato* (Roma 1978). He is vice-president of the Italian Theological Association, and a member of the editorial committee of the Dogma section of *Concilium*.

HENRI-MARIE FÉRET was born on 21 January 1904 in Vannes (France). He became a Dominican on 2 October 1922 and was ordained priest in 1928. He studied philosophy and theology at Le Saulchoir of Belgium and followed a course of study at the Ecole des Hautes-Etudes and the Institut d'Etudes Hispaniques in Paris. He became a doctor of theology in 1930. He taught Church history at Le Saulchoir from 1930 until 1954. From 1943 until 1954 he taught biblical catechesis in various branches of the Institut Catholique in Paris. He was prior of the Dominican community in Dijon between 1958 and 1964. At the Second Vatican Council, he acted as a theologian for the French bishops. Among his publications on the subject of biblical catechesis are: *L'Apocalypse de saint Jean. Vision chrétienne de l'histoire* (1942); *Peuple de Dieu et pâque eucharistique* (1947), which was later adapted and included in *L'Eucharistie, pâque de l'univers* (1966); *Sources bibliques de la pastorale du dimanche* (1948); *La mort dans la tradition biblique* (1951); *Connaissance biblique de Dieu* (1955); *Pierre et Paul à Antioche et à Jérusalem. Le conflit des deux Apôtres* (1955); *Pour une Eglise des béatitudes de la pauvreté* (1965); *La Théologie concrète et historique et son importance pastorale présente* (1974); *Christologie médiévale de saint Thomas et christologie concrète et historique pour aujord'hui* (1975); *Mort et résurrection du Christ d'après les évangiles et d'après le Linceul de Turin* (1980).

JOSEPH KOMONCHAK was born in Nyack, New York in 1939 and ordained in 1963. He studied philosophy at St Joseph's Seminary, Yonkers, NY, and theology at the Gregorian University in Rome, where he received the licentiate in sacred theology in 1964. After serving in a parish for three years, he taught systematic theology at St Joseph's Seminary for ten years. In 1976 he received his doctorate in philosophy at Union Theological Seminary, New York, with a dissertation on the ecclesiology of the young Newman. Since 1977 he has been an associate professor in the Department of Religion and Religious Education at the Catholic University of America, Washington,

DC. He has published articles on ecclesiology, ministry, the theology of liberation, and the ordination of women, in such journals as *The Theological Studies* and *Concilium*.

GEORG KRETSCHMAR was born in 1925 in Landeshut, Schleswig-Holstein. In 1956 he became professor in the Faculty of Protestant Theology in Hamburg and has been professor of Church history and the New Testament in the Faculty of Protestant Theology in Munich since 1967. His work is concerned especially with patristics, reformation and history of the liturgy. He is president of the Protestant Arbeitergemeinschaft für kirchliche Zeitgeschichte, of the Ökumenischen Studienausschusses der Vereinigten Evang. Luth. Kirche Deutschlands, of the Kommission des Luth. Weltbundes für den Dialog mit den Orthodoxen Kirchen. He is at present preparing a commentary on the pastoral letters.

GABRIEL MARC was born in France in 1933. He is a layman, married with five children. He is an administrator with the Institut National de la Statistique et des Etudes Economiques and a former president of the French Catholic Action association for the liberal professions. He is a member of the French Justice and Peace Commission and has a column in the Catholic daily *La Croix*. He has published three books: *Passion pour l'essentiel* (Paris 1975), *La foi du croyant inconnu* (with Geneviève Rivière, Paris 1977), *Qu'ils soient un* (Paris 1978).

MUSHETE NGINDU was born in 1937. He studied at Lovanium University, Kinshasa, Zaïre, and at the Sorbonne. His doctoral thesis was on the religious philosophy of Laberthonnière. He is professor of fundamental theology in the Catholic Theological Faculty at Kinshasa, a founder-member of the Ecumenical Association of Third World Theologians and editor-in-chief of the Association's journal, the *Bulletin de Théologie Africaine*. He has published various studies of Laberthonnière, cultural studies, African Christianity and aspects of theology.

GIUSEPPE RUGGIERI teaches fundamental theology at the S. Paolo Studio Teologico in Catania. He is a member of the Instituto per le scienze Religiose of Bologna and is on the editorial board of this Institute's journal, *Cristianesimo nella storia*. Among his publications we list: *Sapienza e storia. Per una teologia politica della comunita christiana* (Milan 1971); *Chiamata alla verita. Saggia sulla responsabilità della fede e della teologia* (Milan 1975); *La compagnia della fede. Linee di teologia fondamentale* (Turin 1980).

CONCILIUM

Claude Geffré. 0 8164 2542 6 144pp.

The Future of Christian Marriage. Ed. William Bassett and Peter Huizing. 0 8164 2575 2.

Polarization in the Church. Ed. Hans Küng and Walter Kasper. 0 8164 2572 8 156pp.

Spiritual Revivals. Ed. Christian Duquoc and Casiano Floristán. 0 8164 2573 6 156pp.

Power and the Word of God. Ed. Franz Bockle and Jacques Marie Pohier. 0 8164 2574 4 156pp.

The Church as Institution. Ed. Gregory Baum and Andrew Greeley. 0 8164 2575 2 168pp.

Politics and Liturgy. Ed. Herman Schmidt and David Power. 0 8164 2576 0 156pp.

Jesus Christ and Human Freedom. Ed. Edward Schillebeeckx and Bas van Iersel. 0 8164 2577 9 168pp.

The Experience of Dying. Ed. Norbert Greinacher and Alois Müller. 0 8164 2578 7 156pp.

Theology of Joy. Ed. Johannes Baptist Metz and Jean-Pierre Jossua. 0 8164 2579 5 164pp.

The Mystical and Political Dimension of the Christian Faith. Ed. Claude Geffré and Gustavo Guttierez. 0 8164 2580 9 168pp.

The Future of the Religious Life. Ed. Peter Huizing and William Bassett. 0 8164 2094 7 96pp.

Christians and Jews. Ed. Hans Küng and Walter Kasper. 0 8164 2095 5 96pp.

Experience of the Spirit. Ed. Peter Huizing and William Bassett. 0 8164 2096 3 144pp.

Sexuality in Contemporary Catholicism. Ed. Franz Bockle and Jacques Marie Pohier. 0 8164 2097 1 126pp.

Ethnicity. Ed. Andrew Greeley and Gregory Baum. 0 8164 2145 5 120pp.

Liturgy and Cultural Religious Traditions. Ed. Herman Schmidt and David Power. 0 8164 2146 2 120pp.

A Personal God? Ed. Edward Schillebeeckx and Bas van Iersel. 0 8164 2149 8 142pp.

The Poor and the Church. Ed. Norbert Greinacher and Alois Müller. 0 8164 2147 1 128pp.

Christianity and Socialism. Ed. Johannes Baptist Metz and Jean-Pierre Jossua. 0 8164 2148 X 144pp.

The Churches of Africa: Future Prospects. Ed. Claude Geffré and Bertrand Luneau. 0 8164 2150 1 128pp.

Judgement in the Church. Ed. William Bassett and Peter Huizing. 0 8164 2166 8 128pp.

Why Did God Make Me? Ed. Hans Küng and Jürgen Moltmann. 0 8164 2167 6 112pp.

109. **Charisms in the Church.** Ed. Christian Duquoc and Casiano Floristán. 0 8164 2168 4 128pp.

110. **Moral Formation and Christianity.** Ed. Franz Bockle and Jacques Marie Pohier. 0 8164 2169 2 120pp.

111. **Communication in the Church.** Ed. Gregory Baum and Andrew Greeley. 0 8164 2170 6 126pp.

112. **Liturgy and Human Passage.** Ed. David Power and Luis Maldonado. 0 8164 2608 2 136pp.

113. **Revelation and Experience.** Ed. Edward Schillebeeckx and Bas van Iersel. 0 8164 2609 0 134pp.

114. **Evangelization in the World Today.** Ed. Norbert Greinacher and Alois Müller. 0 8164 2610 4 136pp.

115. **Doing Theology in New Places.** Ed. Jean-Pierre Jossua and Johannes Baptist Metz. 0 8164 2611 2 120pp.

116. **Buddhism and Christianity.** Ed. Claude Geffré and Mariasusai Dhavamony. 0 8164 2612 0 136pp.

117. **The Finances of the Church.** Ed. William Bassett and Peter Huizing. 0 8164 2197 8 160pp.

118. **An Ecumenical Confession of Faith?** Ed. Hans Küng and Jürgen Moltmann. 0 8164 2198 6 136pp.

119. **Discernment of the Spirit and of Spirits.** Ed. Casiano Floristán and Christian Duquoc. 0 8164 2199 4 136pp.

120. **The Death Penalty and Torture.** Ed. Franz Bockle and Jacques Marie Pohier. 0 8164 2200 1 136pp.

121. **The Family in Crisis or in Transition.** Ed. Andrew Greely. 0 567 30001 3 128pp.

122. **Structures of Initiation in Crisis.** Ed. Luis Maldonado and David Power. 0 567 30002 1 128pp.

123. **Heaven.** Ed. Bas van Iersel and Edward Schillebeeckx. 0 567 30003 X 120pp.

124. **The Church and the Rights of Man.** Ed. Alois Müller and Norbert Greinacher. 0 567 30004 8 140pp.

125. **Christianity and the Bourgeoisie.** Ed. Johannes Baptist Metz. 0 567 30005 6 144pp.

126. **China as a Challenge to the Church.** Ed. Claude Geffré and Joseph Spae. 0 567 30006 4 136pp.

127. **The Roman Curia and the Communion of Churches.** Ed. Peter Huizing and Knut Walf. 0 567 30007 2 144pp.

128. **Conflicts about the Holy Spirit.** Ed. Hans Küng and Jürgen Moltmann. 0 567 30008 0 144pp.

129. **Models of Holiness.** Ed. Christian Duquoc and Casiano Floristán. 0 567 30009 9 128pp.

130. **The Dignity of the Despised of the Earth.** Ed. Jacques Marie Pohier and Dietmar Mieth. 0 567 30010 2 144pp.

131. **Work and Religion.** Ed. Gregory Baum. 0 567 30011 0 148pp.

132. **Symbol and Art in Worship.** Ed. Luis Maldonado and David Power. 0 567 30012 9 136pp.

133. **Right of the Community to a Priest.** Ed. Edward Schillebeeckx and Johannes Baptist Metz. 0 567 30013 7 148pp.

134. **Women in a Men's Church.** Ed. Virgil Elizondo and Norbert Greinacher. 0 567 30014 5 144pp.

135. **True and False Universality of Christianity.** Ed. Claude Geffré and Jean-Pierre Jossua. 0 567 30015 3 138pp.

136. **What is Religion? An Inquiry for Christian Theology.** Ed. Mircea Eliade and David Tracy. 0 567 30016 1 98pp.

137. **Electing our Own Bishops.** Ed. Peter Huizing and Knut Walf. 0 567 30017 X 112pp.

138. **Conflicting Ways of Interpreting the Bible.** Ed. Hans Küng and Jürgen Moltmann. 0 567 30018 8 112pp.

139. **Christian Obedience.** Ed. Casiano Floristán and Christian Duquoc. 0 567 30019 6 96pp.

140. **Christian Ethics and Economics: the North-South Conflict.** Ed. Dietmar Mieth and Jacques Marie Pohier. 0 567 30020 X 128pp.

1981

141. **Neo-Conservatism: Social and Religious Phenomenon.** Ed. Gregory Baum and John Coleman. 0 567 30021 8.

142. **The Times of Celebration.** Ed. David Power and Mary Collins. 0 567 30022 6.

143. **God and Father.** Ed. Edward Schillebeeckx and Johannes Baptist Metz. 0 567 30023 4.

144. **Tensions Between the Churches of the First World and the Third World.** Ed. Virgil Elizondo and Norbert Greinacher. 0 567 30024 2.

145. **Nietzsche and Christianity.** Ed. Claude Geffré and Jean-Pierre Jossua. 0 567 30025 0.

146. **Where Does the Church Stand?** Ed. Giuseppe Alberigo. 0 567 30026 9.

147. **The Revised Code of Canon Law: a Missed Opportunity?** Ed. Peter Huizing and Knut Walf. 0 567 30027 7.

148. **Who Has the Say in the Church?** Ed. Hans Küng and Jürgen Moltmann. 0 567 30028 5.

149. **Francis of Assisi: an Example?** Ed. Casiano Floristán and Christian Duquoc. 0 567 30029 3.

150. **One Faith, One Church, Many Moralities?** Ed. Jacques Pohier and Dietmar Mieth. 0 567 30030 7.